Listening Prayer

Mary Ruth Swope

Listening Prayer

Dr. Mary Ruth Swope
P.O. Box 1746
Melbourne, Florida, 32901

Copyright © 1987 by Dr. Mary Ruth Swope
Printed in the United States of America
ISBN: 0-88368-193-5

Editorial assistance by Valeria Cindric

Unless otherwise noted, Scripture quotations are taken from the *King James Version* of the Bible.

DEDICATION

This book is dedicated, first of all, to those hungry souls who are faithful to seek the Lord, ask Him for His wisdom and guidance, and continually knock on heaven's door "that they might know . . . the only true God, and Jesus Christ. . . ." (John 17:3).

Secondly, I would like to dedicate this book to my two children, Stephen and Susan, who share with me the vision of helping believers and unbelievers shape up both spiritually and physically.

Next, this book is dedicated to my husband, Don, who has stood with me, prayed with me, and sought the Lord's will with me throughout its conception, writing, and final publication.

Lastly, and most importantly, I wish to dedicate this work to my Inspiration, my Guide, and my Friend—the Lord Jesus Christ—who has created the desire in me to "publish with the voice of thanksgiving, and tell of all [His] wondrous works" (Psalm 26:7).

ACKNOWLEDGMENTS

Excerpts from the following publications are quoted in this book and used with permission of the publishers:

Carnal Christians and Other Words That Don't Go Together by Rich Wilkerson. Whitaker House, Springdale, Pennsylvania, 1986.

God Did Nor Ordain Silence by Christopher Christianson. Logos International, Plainfield, New Jersey, 1974.

Hudson Taylor in Early Years: The Growth of a Soul by Dr. and Mrs. Howard Taylor. The China Inland Mission, London.

Is That Really You, God? by Loren Cunningham. Chosen Books, Grand Rapids, Michigan, 1984.

Memoirs of Rev. Charles G. Finney by Charles G. Finney. The A. S. Barnes Company, New York, 1876.

My God Will Supply by Dede Robertson. Chosen Books, Lincoln, Virginia, 1979.

My Life Without God by William Murray. Thomas Nelson Publishers, New York, 1982.

Shaping History Through Prayer and Fasting by Derek Prince. Fleming H. Revell Company, Old Tappan, New Jersey, 1979.

Scripture quotations marked *TLB* are from *The Living Bible*. Copyright © 1971 by Tyndale House Publishers, Wheaton Illinois. Used by permission.

CONTENTS

INTRODUCTION

"Believe it or not," the prayer seminar speaker said, "God wants to speak to you personally every day about the affairs of your life."

At that time, I had been a born-again Christian for forty-one years. But I had never been presented with the idea of listening to God for personal guidance and inspiration. Often I had heard Christian leaders say, "The Lord told me . . ." or "God said to me . . ." or "The Holy Spirit spoke and told me such and such." But the idea that God was willing to speak regularly to *me*, a "layman," was news indeed.

I set out to prove for myself whether or not this could really be true. My subsequent wrestling with the speaker's contention—through a study of the Word and by following his recommendation to listen in prayer—changed my life and led me to write this book.

Listening prayer is *not* a new discovery or a recent innovation. It isn't even a new slant on an old discovery! It is a time-honored and proven method of hearing from God that is almost totally ignored by modern-day Christians.

Believers who seek friendship with God through listening experiences discover greater direction and purpose for their lives. They are the ones who are then transformed and anointed for greater service in the Kingdom of God.

Listening prayer, of course, is just one facet of prayer. It is *not* a quick-fix to all our problems. It is, however, one neglected weapon in God's arsenal that will help us find His path through life's perplexing maze.

Let me encourage you to begin a regular program of listening prayer. Add it to your list of personal disciplines needed for successful Christian living.

My prayer is that as God challenged me through a seminar speaker to make listening prayer a regular part of my daily quiet time, so He will challenge you through the reading of this book.

CHAPTER ONE
Life-Changing Experiences

My first year of college was spent at a small, church-related institution. During my first week of classes, I attended a revival meeting for new students and had a life-changing spiritual experience at an old-fashioned altar service. I repented of my sins and invited Jesus Christ to be my Savior.

From what did He save me? It would take another book to tell you fully. But during the twenty years following my graduation from college, my faith in God kept me from giving up in spite of financial lack, much sickness, constant emotional pain, and deep sorrow. The Lord was faithful to keep me from severe bodily harm, emotional despair, and ultimate defeat.

When the tragedies in my life eventually compounded and made my situation unbearable, I became truly hungry and thirsty to *know* God personally. This time my hunger was greater than a fleeting impulse to hear *about* God. My situation demanded more than another sermon or teaching—more than drinking at the traditional religious trough on Sundays.

In searching for power to overcome my problems, I did all the usual things: I read books; I talked with pastors; I attended conferences and read my Bible regularly. Many people knew that I had a desperate need for guidance from God. Yet no one in my circle of Christian friends encouraged me by word or by example to "be still" and let God speak to me.

A closer walk with God, I was taught, resulted from regular church attendance, being active in every church function, reading the Bible every day, and saying my prayers. In fact, these are the main methods I had used to grow in grace and in the knowledge of the Truth for the first forty-one years of my Christian life.

I also heard weekly sermons on the restrictions placed on today's saints. If I wanted to be truly holy and sanctified, I must never attend a movie, wear earrings, or use cosmetics. Dancing and card playing were forbidden; and if you were a girl, you couldn't play baseball or knit on Sunday. The list was interminable and depended, of course, upon the denomination of the church I was attending at the time.

My pastors and teachers were motivated by good intentions, desiring to keep me "unspotted from the world." But by "majoring on minors" and neglecting to lead me into righteousness by the only way that works—namely, to *know* God personally—they were a great deterrent to my spiritual growth.

Man-made rules and regulations create bigoted, self-righteous people instead of true men and women of God. In addition, they cheat Christians out of experiencing sustained peace and true tranquillity of spirit. What a pity.

But God is always faithful. If we sincerely desire to be guided by Him, we *will* be.

The Seminar That Changed My World

God led me along spiritually one step at a time—always encouraging me to "press on." He kept me from falling until He sent across my path a teacher who could share with me the secret to Christian maturity that I was lacking.

The answer came during a weekend seminar called *Change the World School of Prayer.* Although my original intention for attending was to learn how to pray effectively, the Lord had a deeper lesson in mind for me.

The seminar leader began with these words: "This is *not* a seminar to teach you how to pray," the leader said. "This is a seminar to teach you what prayer is, how prayer works, what the scriptures say about prayer, some examples of answered prayer, and the like. The way to learn to pray is by praying. Practice makes perfect in prayer as in any other skill to be mastered."

At first I was disappointed. But little did I realize that this seminar would ultimately lead to a dramatic change in my life—one that will help me to change from glory to glory as long as I live.

Prayer was defined as *communication with God*. It was pointed out that communication, to be effective, must be between at least two people. No satisfying fellowship or genuine friendship can be expected to develop when one person does all the talking while the other simply listens. This is true on the human level, as any marriage counselor can verify, and it is also true in the spiritual realm—in our communication with God.

This idea brought an expansion of my thinking about who God really is and about my personal friendship with Him. I realized that I had been praying for years to a vague God "way out there in the heavens somewhere." My only thought or expectation in prayer had been to encourage Him to help me achieve the goals I had set for myself.

During the seminar, it became apparent to me that my habits in prayer were out of line with God's Word. My prayers were almost totally devoted to asking God for favors for myself, my family members, and my friends.

Friendship With God

The challenge made at the seminar was simple, short, and clear. "Not literally, but figuratively," our leader said, "spend 51% of your prayer time in listening prayer. Ask God if He has anything to share with you, or ask Him a question and then sit in His presence waiting for an answer." We were assured that every believer could have a genuine encounter with God and receive direct guidance for our lives.

The seminar leader said that God is a Person whose friendship can be cultivated as any other person's can be. God hears us every time we talk to Him. Because He loves, cares, and feels, God delights in sharing with His children. He has many ways of communicating with His creation, especially those made in His very own image. He communicates with us through our spirit and soul—our will and emotions. His communication is continuous and done in love, with our best interests in mind. Thus, even stern correction and God's words of admonition are treasures of blessing.

For the first time in my life, I learned that God wants to speak to each one of us personally. He spoke to the prophets and apostles; the scriptural record from one end of the Bible to the other proves it. But God also wants to speak today. His voice and His desire to speak are not dispensational; they are for all of God's children in every generation and in any age.

My simple faith could accept that teaching. Since God is portrayed in Scripture as a communicator, would it not bring glory to Him for me to receive personal direction for my life? After all, He made me, and He is the only One who knows what accomplishments I was created to achieve.

Armed only with this teaching from a two-day seminar on prayer—the kind of prayer that changes the world—I began to spend time almost daily in what I have grown to call "listening prayer." My hearty pursuit of friendship with God achieved the promised results: I began to hear Him speak!

Drawing Near

No amount of right theology and right keeping of the law (ancient or modern) can do for your spirit what hearing directly from God about your personal problems and concerns can. In addition, His conversations often extend beyond our own little world to speak of global problems and universal truths.

This manifestation of truth can make a powerful difference in a believer's life. One is changed from being a nominal Christian who lacks power to one who does great exploits for God.

Drawing near to God always causes God to come nearer to us. This experience of being close to God is not a special gift offered to only a few. Jesus said, "*All* who are of the truth hear my voice" (John 18:37, *italics added*). A. W. Tozer said it so well when he wrote: "All God has done for *any* of His children He will do for *all* of His children."

If you have any desire at all to get close to God, begin to fan the spark even if it is only a flicker. Open up your heart to Him and start sharing your deepest longings and needs. As you draw close to God, He will manifest Himself in special ways with the sweetness of His presence.

Opening Up the Channel

I have often wondered why I was unable to discover this great truth of listening prayer on my own. It wasn't until I faced certain facts about my spiritual life that the answer was revealed to me. First of all,

I realized that, even though I was a true Christian, my heart was not seeking after God. Instead, I was seeking after success and glory in the world system. The soulish pursuits of money, prestige, professional power, and possessions kept me totally preoccupied until just a few years ago.

In addition, I did not allocate enough time for God. I was too busy and too comfortable pursuing self-interests. My fleshly lusts were unjudged and uncrucified, and they dominated and exploited my time, talents, ideas, values, and money.

If you can identify with the way I was and you want to be changed, ask God to help you. Pray: "Lord show me how to accept the suffering of 'dying to self.' Show me how to be set free from self in order to worship only You. Stay with me while I put myself on the cross. When I am resurrected to new life in Christ, fill me up with Yourself by Your power and for Your glory."

This is a difficult but necessary task. As you go through this ordeal of self-crucifixion, the presence of the Living God will be very near. Then two-way communication between you and God will flow naturally. Once the channel has been unstopped, God stands ready to let His "still small voice" flow freely with astounding clarity and perfection.

The Place Of Prayer

The place where listening prayer takes place is also crucial to hearing from God—at least when you are a beginner. It is difficult to hear God's voice in the kitchen with three toddlers screaming for your attention or in the family room with the television blaring at you. Even a quieter place like your bedroom may not be best if you can be interrupted by another family member. My personal experience is that listening prayer is easiest when done alone with the door shut.

This is what Jesus taught. He told His disciples, "But when you pray, go away by yourself, all alone, and shut the door behind you and pray to your Father secretly, and your Father, who knows your secrets, will reward you" (Matthew 6:6, *TLB*).

For the first forty-one years of my Christian life, I prayed in a multitude of places and in a variety of posture positions. But not once did I try the command of Jesus—to pray behind a closed door. At the prayer seminar where I learned about listening prayer, the concept of a prayer closet was introduced. The leader gave illustrations from the lives of people who had experienced many miracles in their lives after learning to pray in their prayer closet.

Before leaving the seminar, I envisioned my own "new place" of prayer—a downstairs closet not needed by present family members. As soon as I returned home, I emptied the closet, made a place to sit, and, with my Bible before me, began to pray there. The moment I closed the door and looked around in the darkness of the closet, I knew I would make progress. The stillness, the lack of sight, and the privacy would enable me to pray in greater depth and with more honesty and fervor than before. And that is exactly what happened.

As the weeks and months went by, I found myself excited about praying. Instead of being a duty, prayer became a joy. I could see new and greater things happening as a result of my secret place. Since establishing a prayer closet ten years ago, I have experienced more spiritual growth than in all the forty-one previous years of my Christian walk.

In his book, *Carnal Christians and Other Words That Don't Go Together,* Pastor Rich Wilkerson recalls an incident involving Dick Eastman, founder and director of "Change the World School of Prayer."

Dick has been used by God to motivate multitudes of people to pray. When I was a twelve-year-old boy, Dick and his wife Delores, who is my cousin, came from North Central Bible College to be my father's youth pastors. Dick was twenty years old then. Because of his influence on those kids, many learned the power of prayer and were changed by God's touch.

One summer while my parents were on vacation, I stayed with Dick and Dee. They had a little, fifteen-year-old, wiped-out trailer home. It was so small they could hardly turn around in it. I mean it was small. Dick was finishing his schooling at the university and holding down a full-time job as the youth minister. One morning around 3:00 a.m., I got up to go to the bathroom. The door was partially opened, and a light was on. I pushed the door a little to see why the light was on. There was Dick using the only private place in the trailer as his prayer closet. Each night that week, at 3:00 a.m., Dick prayed on his knees in his "prayer closet."

Your prayer closet doesn't have to be a fancy built-on addition to your home; it can be any place where you will not be disturbed. If you have not already done so, immediately find a quiet area—preferably a small, dark place—where you can enter in, close the door, and pray verbally to God in secret. You will quickly discover that Jesus had our highest good in mind when He gave this command about the place needed for effective prayer.

This life-changing experience awaits you. Don't miss the opportunity to change your world through a personal prayer encounter with Almighty God in your prayer closet.

Arise And Come Away

One day I was meditating on 1 Peter 2:7, "The same Stone that was rejected by the builders has become the Cornerstone" (*TLB*). I wondered, What does this mean for contemporary Christians? Would it ever be possible for the Head Corner to be rejected? Under what conditions might this happen? Is it possible for me to reject the Head Corner in my Christian walk? By not listening to God's voice, am I rejecting Him?

As I considered this, I heard the Lord say:

"My daughter, I still speak to any child of Mine who will humble herself and listen. I do not shout over the daily turmoil sounds of the average household. Oh no! My voice is not weak, but it is quiet, calm, and serene. It takes complete surrender on your part before you can hear it. That surrender must be complete—body, soul, and spirit surrender.

"Furthermore, I do not answer casual inquiries. It is only those who are persistent in wanting to communicate *with* Me who hear, not the excitement-seekers or the stubborn fool who sets out to prove or disprove My ability and My willingness to talk. Faith coupled with humility and persistence brings results.

"I am perfectly willing and capable of revealing Who I am to anyone who truly wants to know. Lay aside all previous knowledge and understanding. Blank your mind like you would erase a blackboard for a new lesson. Wash it perfectly clean. Then come directly to Me and ask that I would write with My chalk to give a new lesson, a fresh lecture, if you please, that would take you beyond the last one revealed.

"All I ask is that you seek for yourself. Trust Me to show, tell, reveal, and embellish."

Let that be the Lord's special word to you. He's calling for you to join Him in sweet communion, "Arise, my love, my fair one, and come away" (Solomon's Song 2:13). Don't keep God waiting.

CHAPTER TWO

God Is Calling Your Name

Is it possible to hear God's voice today? More specifically, is it possible for *every* Christian to hear God's voice? Can we actually receive answers from God to specific questions about how to proceed in the circumstances prevailing in our daily lives?

If you thought the answer to that question was "yes," wouldn't you be motivated to seek God's counsel and advice more often about more situations and more people? Of course you would!

Modern man has been taught that he is capable of solving his problems by himself and standing on his own two feet. In fact, most professional psychologists, psychiatrists, doctors, and even some ministers discredit and discourage our need for help from a higher power. They ignore the experiences of men and women who have delved into a deep relationship with God and found such help.

In America, the wide acceptance of humanism has created a dependence upon secularly trained professionals. When we have a problem or an important decision to make, it is seldom suggested that we personally seek God's advice for the solution or ask Him for specific guidance. Instead, we are usually advised to talk to our pastor, our doctor, a psychologist, the boss, or our spouse—but never God. Anyone who talks or writes about a personal encounter with God and seeks Him as the ultimate source of guidance and counsel is often viewed as "abnormal" or out of step with the times.

So why am I plunging ahead to share my deepest and most intimate experiences with God? The answer is simple. Learning to hear God speak to me personally through the Holy Spirit has been the most exciting, thrilling, and exhilarating experience of my whole life.

Living In Power

The most fruitful and satisfying time of my life has been those years since I learned to hear God's voice. Receiving and following God's guidance has led me down exciting paths that my feet would otherwise have never touched. Again and again His wisdom and counsel have made this business of daily living the super-satisfying, abundant life Jesus promised.

This being true, I am willing to go against the mainstream of modern thought and action in an attempt to help others find joy in using this divinely ordained tool for successful living. Every person-in-Christ needs and can have a listening-hearing experience with God that will enable them to *live in power.*

Ordinary people can and do experience God personally. When this relationship is developed over time, living in power becomes the norm for God's children. Yes, the *norm*. Living in power, in authority, and in victory is God's perfect plan. His offer of divine guidance—made possible through listening prayer—is *one* of the ways He enables us to fulfill His plan for our individual lives and accomplish His purpose in the world.

When I was a university administrator, many times the Lord enabled me to discharge my duties with an efficiency I could never have produced on my own. At other times He gave me a gift of revelation about how to proceed in a certain situation.

One morning I went to work at the university very early—an hour before secretaries were due there. At that time in my career, I was having a difficult relationship problem with a faculty member. In my desk file drawer there was a folder—"unlabeled" and filed at random—containing my personal notes made during conferences with faculty. The folder was "dynamite" because I often wrote my frustrations on paper to rid myself of the hostility I sometimes felt. Needless to say, I wanted to keep those thoughts private.

When I arrived at school, I looked for the file, but it was missing. My heart literally jumped. When my first secretary came to work, I asked her if she had seen the file. She was indignant and said, "Dean Swope, you know I never get in your personal file drawer. Why would you accuse me of that?" I apologized, but she was still very upset.

Then the second secretary arrived. I asked the same question of her. She was not as upset by my question, but she told me in no uncertain terms that I should have known better than to ask her such a thing. Now I was more nervous than ever.

I told the two girls that I needed to go home—knowing that I was headed for my prayer closet. God knew who had the folder, and I believed that He would tell me. Within forty-five minutes, I felt that the Lord had given me the name of the person who had removed the folder.

With confidence, I returned to school, knowing I had heard correctly. When I approached the person in her office, she denied it, saying, "Why Dean Swope, you know I would not do such a thing as that." To which I replied, "On the highest authority there is, I know that you did and I want it right now." She grabbed her purse, left the office, and in twenty minutes was back with the folder.

My problem was solved, or at least partially. She may have read all of my notes, but they were still in the folder and to my knowledge there were no repercussions from what she had learned by reading them. You see, I needed personal guidance—and God gave it to me—on time!

The Distinguishing Mark

In his cassette tape series, *Hearing God's Voice*, Derek Prince says that God has dealt with the human race in different ways throughout specific periods of history. We know this from the three dispensations revealed in the Bible: *the time of the Patriarchs* (fathers of families); *the dispensation of the Law* that was given for Israel; and then, last, *the dispensation of the Gospel*, a proclamation to the whole human race that requires an individual response. We are still living in this third dispensation.

Dr. Prince makes the point that there was only one unvarying characteristic of God's people throughout all of these dispensations—*they heard the voice of God*. This, he said, was the distinguishing mark that made those who belonged to God different from those who did not. Receiving divine guidance was absolutely necessary for finding their place in God's plan. The same is true for today's believers.

The Old Testament is filled with stories of individuals who were given explicit directions from God. Abram was told to leave his country and relatives and go to a place where God would lead him. (See Genesis 12:1.) God spoke to Jacob and told him to return to his homeland. (See Genesis 31:3.) Others were given specific instructions regarding finding a wife, assuming leadership, waging war, obtaining supplies, anointing leaders, and pronouncing judgments.

As we read the stories in the Old Testament, we find that God gave specific guidance for many perplexing situations: for business affairs (Genesis 31:1-16); in battle (Joshua 6:1-21); in great emergencies (2 Kings 2:19-22); for the childless couple (Judges 13:1-25); and about the teachings of the scriptures (2 Kings 22:13).

> Long ago God spoke in many different ways to our fathers through the prophets [in visions, dreams, and even face to face], telling them little by little about his plans. But now in these days he has spoken to us through his Son to whom he has given everything, and through whom he made the world and everything there is—Hebrews 1:1-2, *TLB*.

Throughout history God has continued to speak to His children. The New Testament is replete with illustrations of those who heard directly from God about specific situations in their lives. Simeon was told by the Holy Ghost that he would not see death before he had seen the Lord Christ. (See Luke 2:26.) Peter was told that three men would come to see him and that he should go with them because they were sent by God (See Acts 11:11,12.)

The writings of the apostle Paul make it unmistakably clear that he frequently received guidance for his daily life. He said, "I was not called to be a missionary by any group or agency. My call is from Jesus Christ himself, and from God the Father" (Galatians 1:1, *TLB*). At another time he said, "I went [to Jerusalem] with definite orders from God" (Galatians 2:2, *TLB*). He told others, "I advise you to obey the Holy Spirit's instructions. He will tell you where to go and what to do." (Galatians 5:16, *TLB*).

How did Paul receive these instructions? He answers that question himself. Paul said that the Lord Jesus Christ gives the spirit of wisdom and

revelation by His Holy Spirit to enlighten our understanding that we might know what God wants us to
do. (See Ephesians 1:17 and 3:3.)

The question that concerns us in our generation
is whether or not God is still speaking. Is He still
giving divine revelation to His children in the form
of visions, dreams, the "still small voice," etc. I
believe the answer is: "absolutely yes."

Why God Wants To Speak To Us

Here is a list of some of the reasons God wants
to speak to His children today:

> To guide us into all truth—John 16:13.
> To guide us in the midst of
> uncertainties—Isaiah 42:16.
> So our soul will live—Isaiah 55:3.
> That we may be guided by wise
> counsel—Psalm 73:24.
> So we can warn others, as prophets do—
> Ezekiel 33:7.

God wants us to hear from Him so He can help
us live victoriously. Jesus said, "The words that I
speak unto you, they are spirit, and they are life"
(John 6:63). Great success awaits those whose soul's
desire is to hear from heaven on all the crucial
matters of life.

One time during a praise service, as I was standing with my arms uplifted in worship, I heard the
Lord call me by name. As I listened, He began to

speak to me. Quickly, I sat down, got a note pad from my purse, and began to write what the Lord was saying to me. When I had finished recording this powerful message, the Lord told me I was not to share it at this particular time but to present it the next time I spoke before an audience. Little did I know that within two hours I would be given the opportunity to stand before a group of seven hundred people. When I shared the message God had given me, it was the "perfect word" for that occasion.

God is calling you by name, and He wants you to hear Him. Why would God call us by name and want us to hear Him speak? Because *God works through individuals.* It has been said that God writes history in terms of human personality. If that is indeed true, then how can we fulfill God's purpose for this life without communicating with Him about His plan for us? How can we get answers to our everyday questions? The truth is—we can't!

If I am willing to listen in prayer, I can receive creative instructions, as well as some remarkable secrets, for my personal affairs. David wrote, "My soul, wait thou only upon God; for my expectation is from him. He only is my rock and my salvation: he is my defence; I shall not be moved" (Psalm 62:5-6). When we wait on God, we can expect to receive words that will encourage, bless, and protect us.

Charting Our Path

When our spirit communicates with the Spirit of God, we give ourselves to the highest level of communion possible. God, after all, knows more about us than we do ourselves. David wrote in the Psalms:

> O Lord, you have examined my heart and know everything about me. You know when I sit or stand. When far away you know my every thought. You chart the path ahead of me, and tell me where to stop and rest. Every moment, you know where I am. You know what I am going to say before I say it. You both precede and follow me, and place your hand of blessing on my head— Psalm 139:1-5, *TLB*.

Corrie Ten Boom in her book, *Tramp for the Lord*, gives an example of how we can trust God to chart the course for our lives.

> My last stop on my first trip to the Orient was Formosa. It was time for me to move on so I went to the travel agency in Taipei and gave the girl a list of all the places I needed to go on the next leg of my journey. Hong Kong, Sydney, Auckland, then back to Sydney, on to Cape Town, Tel Aviv and finally to Amsterdam. . . .
> I left the travel agency with a good feeling in my heart. Surely God was going to bless this trip since I was already off to such a good start. However, when I arrived in my room and checked my ticket, I found

the girl had made a mistake in the route. Instead of sending me from Sydney to Cape Town to Tel Aviv, as I had requested, she had routed me from Sydney to Tel Aviv and then to Cape Town. I went immediately to the phone and called her.

"Why have you changed my schedule?" I asked. "My Chief has told me I must go first to Cape Town and after that to Tel Aviv. However, you have changed the sequence. God is my Master and I must obey Him."

"Then God has made a mistake," she said, half-seriously. "There is no direct flight from Australia to Africa since there is no island in the Indian Ocean for the plane to land and refuel. That is why you must first go overland to Tel Aviv and then down to Cape Town."

"No," I argued. "I cannot follow that route. I must do what my Chief has told me. I'll just have to pray for an island in the Indian Ocean."

We both laughed and hung up. "Lord," I prayed, "if I have made a mistake in hearing Your direction, please show me. But if I heard correctly, then open the way."

An hour later the girl called back. "Did you really pray for an island in the Indian Ocean?" she asked, incredulous. Before I could answer she continued, "I have just received a telegram from Quantas, the Australian Airline. They have just begun to use the Cocos Islands for a refueling station and beginning tomorrow will have a direct flight from Sydney to Cape Town."

I thanked her and hung up. It was good to know that God does not make a mistake in His plans.

God wants to show us the course He has charted for our lives. As we learn to hear His voice, we can move and rest according to His timetable—not ours. Knowing when to act and when to wait before taking action can keep us from making many tragic and unprofitable mistakes. "A man is a fool to trust himself! But those who use God's wisdom are safe" (Proverbs 28:26, *TLB*).

When the prophet Jeremiah needed specific instructions for a given situation, God told him, "Ask me and I will tell you some remarkable secrets about what is going to happen here" (Jeremiah 33:3, *TLB*). God knows the present and future details of our lives, and He is willing to share them with us—if we will only ask.

Unordained Silence

One way God's will is made known to us is by the voice of the Holy Spirit. Jesus made it clear that the Holy Spirit would be our teacher and give us guidance and direction. (See John 14:17.) The same is true today. The inner voice of the Holy Spirit will guide and direct us.

Since we know that God dwells within us, isn't it reasonable to expect Him to speak to us from within? This makes *hearing* a matter of spirit communion— from God's Spirit to our spirit. The need to hear an "audible voice," therefore, is eliminated. God can speak audibly if He so desires, but most guidance from God comes from within and not by a voice that others could hear or that a cassette tape could record.

Christopher Christianson, a Lutheran pastor, tells in his book, *God Did Not Ordain Silence,* how God clearly spoke to him one day:

> Several years ago, as I stretched out in our reclining chair for a catnap after lunch, I heard a voice say, "God did not ordain silence." I had not begun to doze, having barely started to relax when the voice spoke. I heard the voice clearly. It was distinct and abrupt. And audible. But no one else was in the room.
>
> At first I was puzzled and prayed for enlightenment. It was too easy to interpret a supernatural message to mean what one wanted it to mean, like the Israelites of old who interpreted so much prophecy the wrong way.
>
> The true meaning . . . gradually became clearer to my mind. . . . As I prayed, an inner voice informed me, "As a loving Father, I want to speak to My children, but they do not listen to Me. Tell My people to listen, for I would speak with them."

God's Spirit communicates to our spirit just like Jesus said He would: "When the Holy Spirit, who is truth, comes, he shall guide you into all truth, for he will not be presenting his own ideas, but will be passing on to you what he has heard. He will tell you about the future" (John 16:13, *TLB*).

Jesus told us what kinds of messages we can expect to hear. He said that the Holy Spirit would guide us into all truth. We can expect all truth because the Holy Spirit is not speaking to us of Himself, but what He hears from God. And God, Jesus said, will show us things to come.

God shares His thoughts about our present and future circumstances by letting us have "fresh words" from heaven. When He communicates these to us, our spirit "bears witness" to what the Holy Spirit is saying, and we know we have heard God's "still small voice."

God is calling your name. Are you listening?

CHAPTER THREE

Becoming A Listener

Anyone can recite prayers, make personal requests, petition for others, intercede, and praise the Lord. But usually it takes more than a "casual relationship" with God to *hear* His voice.

We can pray in many different ways. There are prayers of petition, intercession, supplication, praise, and listening prayer—to name a few. While all effective prayer begins with knowing God through Jesus Christ, listening prayer has certain prerequisites not required by other kinds of praying.

"My sheep hear my voice and I know them, and they follow me" (John 10:27). The sheep spoken of by Jesus walk and talk with the Shepherd, constantly enjoying His presence and listening for His voice. God's Son (the Shepherd) desires to communicate with all His sheep (the true believers). But are we listening?

Some Christians are unwilling to be still before the Lord and listen to hear His voice. "They have hardened their hearts like flint, afraid to hear the words that God, the Lord of Hosts commanded them. . . . I called but they refused to listen" (Zechariah 7:12,13, *TLB*).

Why won't many believers give God an opportunity to speak to them? Because they are afraid of what He will say. They fail to realize that their loving heavenly Father longs to have a personal relationship with them that will bring great blessing to their lives.

God will not force His way into our hearts or shout His commands into our ears. Like a patient, gentle Father, God waits for us to open our hearts and our ears. "Behold, I stand at the door, and knock: if any man hear my voice, and open the door, I will come in to him, and will sup with him, and he with me" (Revelation 3:20).

Communion with God in prayer is the high privilege of every believer who delights in fellowship with the Almighty. Listening, however, is an art that must be cultivated and developed. It is God's business to speak to us, and it is our business to be still and listen.

Your Undivided Attention

Listening prayer requires an intimate friendship with God—a relationship that demands your full attention and much quiet time spent alone with Him. And that is not an easy task. Giving God one's undivided attention for a protracted length of time is difficult.

Fretting or worrying about things to be done, people to be served, and tasks to be finished can distract us and interfere with our ability to listen to God. This gospel incident involving the two sisters, Mary and Martha, provides a vivid contrast between fretting and listening.

> As Jesus and the disciples continued on their way to Jerusalem they came to a village where a woman named Martha welcomed them into her home. Her sister Mary sat on the floor, listening to Jesus as he talked.
>
> But Martha was the jittery type, and was worrying over the big dinner she was preparing.
>
> She came to Jesus and said, "Sir, doesn't it seem unfair to you that my sister just sits here while I do all the work? Tell her to come and help me."
>
> But the Lord said to her, "Martha, dear friend, you are so upset over all these details! There is really only one thing worth being concerned about. Mary has discovered it—and I won't take it away from her!"—Luke 10:38-42, *TLB*.

When I first began taking time to listen to God, it was difficult for me to clear away thoughts about my daily agenda. I soon learned to keep a pad and pen nearby so I could write down "to-do items."

This freed my mind from trying to remember many little details and enabled me to give my full attention to the Lord.

Quieting Your Soul

True intimacy with God cannot be realized without total *quietness* of body, mind, and spirit. And that requires scheduling adequate time to be alone in His presence. An atmosphere of quietness is absolutely essential for listening prayer. "Be still and know that I am God" (Psalm 46:10) is a command we need to obey and put into practice in our prayer life.

Sometimes God will speak while we are working or thinking. At other times it is necessary that we are totally relaxed and silent. We often think that by keeping busy we are doing the will of God, but the Holy Spirit once spoke to me and said, "It is not activity that counts, but following My orders."

At the beginning of each period of listening prayer, submit yourself to God and invite the Holy Spirit to be in control. Learn to put your mind on the shelf. If your own thoughts begin to seep through, you will block the Holy Spirit's willingness to speak through your mind.

In addition, Satan will try to distract you. Cast out any interfering thoughts from the enemy. The clamoring images and mindset of the world will drown out the quiet inner promptings of the Holy Spirit.

Sit back and enjoy God's presence. Meditate on His power, His wisdom, His goodness, His meekness, and

His generosity. Let His peace flow through you, and feel the serenity of mind and heart that illuminates and invigorates. His Spirit gives strength to any task that needs to be accomplished.

Learn to relax and release all tension. Anxiety and strain will evoke only silence from God. Learn to let go and let God speak to you.

David summed it up when he wrote, "Rest in the Lord; wait patiently for Him to act . . . Don't fret or worry. . . . All who humble themselves before the Lord shall be given many blessings, and shall have wonderful peace" (Psalm 37:7,8,11, *TLB*).

Only those who retreat to the quietness of heart, mind, and spirit can hear God's voice and receive direct inspiration.

Patient Expectancy

Another requirement for developing true intimacy with God in prayer is *patience*. God wants His children to develop the holy art of waiting upon Him. And that may mean waiting and waiting and waiting! Listening prayer is one of the workshops God uses to teach us this priceless fruit of the Spirit— patience.

The determination to be persistent in listening to God, when coupled with a thankful heart, can work miracles in your life. Fortitude and gratitude, though distinctly separate words, are inextricably linked in a prayer-closet experience. Both are often present at the end of a busy day and a busy week. It takes real fortitude to bring one to dedicated prayer and praise. Yet, many times it is gratitude that releases the fortitude.

The psalmist was in no hurry. He said, "Lead me in thy truth, and teach me: for thou art the God of my salvation; on thee do I wait all the day" (Psalm 25:5).

Let me ask you a question. Do you find it easy to wait on your friends or family members? Most likely your answer is the same as mine: "No, I don't!" But let me tell you that waiting on the Lord is more difficult than waiting for yourself or your friends to act.

I listened regularly for one year before I heard anything from God. When, at last, I began hearing that "still small voice" I immediately recognized it as being from God.

Listening for God to speak to us also requires an *expectant attitude.* Unless we believe that God wants to speak to us, and unless we are willing to wait for Him to do so, we will not experience the joys of listening prayer. Although you may have to wait for hours, you soon learn that the rewards of hearing from Him are always exhilarating.

Rich Wilkerson tells about a time when he was seeking direction for his life. He had received a call to become youth pastor at his uncle's church in Fort Worth, Texas, but Rich, then only nineteen, had answered that he was "too young." After his uncle encouraged him to pray and ask God to help him make the right decision, however, Rich agreed to seek the Lord.

I prayed for eleven days—sought God on my knees every night and every morning. For all eleven days, it seemed the windows of heaven were shut. On the eleventh night, I asked my roommate to pray with me. . . .

After about thirty minutes of lying flat out on my face before God, I once again sensed the voice of the Holy Spirit. . . .

By now I knew enough to ask for *scriptural confirmation*. The Lord led me to the first chapter of Jeremiah that describes the call of God upon the life of the young prophet. Many theologians believe he may have been between the ages of sixteen and twenty-two at the time.

The Word of God came to Jeremiah saying, "Before I formed thee in the belly I knew thee; and before thou cameth forth out of the womb I sanctified thee, and I ordained thee a prophet unto the nations." And Jeremiah answered, "Ah, Lord God! behold, I cannot speak: for I am a child" (Jeremiah 1:5-6).

That's what I was telling God. Isn't it wild that God chose to show me another young man in history that had been going through the same struggle!

I answered the call of God that night—called my uncle and said, "I'm coming!"

Don't tell me God doesn't speak to us directly. I want you to know God hears and *answers* prayer. Even though that incident happened years ago in my life, it's as fresh in my memory as if it happened yesterday.

Rich Wilkerson's patient expectancy paid off. And time has proved that Rich definitely heard from God that day. His dynamic ministry to youth and single adults has brought thousands into the Kingdom and made many disciples for Jesus Christ.

Putting God First

The psalmist wrote, "O God, thou art my God; early will I seek thee" (Psalm 63:1). Many other passages in the Bible indicate that seeking God early was a common practice of godly men and women. Even Jesus found it necessary to get up early before His disciples and retreat to a place where He could spend time communing with His Father.

I once heard a well-known pastor say that he was taught from early childhood, "No Bible, no breakfast."

The Lord longs for us to spend time with Him before our minds are heavily committed with things we need to do. If we come to Him when we first get up, before we go about our day's activities, He will direct our steps and keep us out of Satan's rut-holes. As we walk our daily paths of service and pleasure, blessings will follow us.

Once in a listening-prayer experience, I heard God speak these words through the Holy Spirit: "Any child of mine who puts Me first can have My best."

Putting the Father first by spending time in prayer before—not after—we are deep into the day's activities, will assure us of His perfect guidance and direction.

You have all day! Give the best hours to God, and He will use the leftovers in miraculous ways to accomplish His purposes better than you could have done by giving your work first priority.

During one of my early morning times with the Lord, I heard Him say,

> "Today is an open book before you. I want to fill it with meaningful, rewarding experiences. Your pathway will be lightened from beginning to end because you have sought divine guidance early in the day."

While there are many distractions and deterrents to hearing God's voice in a listening-prayer experience, I hope the special rewards of hearing will fire you with enthusiasm to become a listener and take time to hear God speak to you.

CHAPTER FOUR

How God Speaks Today

Soon after I began listening and hearing the voice of the Holy Spirit speaking sentences into my mind, I told one of my dearest friends about the experience. I wanted her to hear God's voice, too, but she said, "Oh, I can see why the Lord would speak to *you*. You've been a faithful believer such a long time and have been praying and witnessing and trying hard to be a good Christian. But He would never speak to *me*. I'm much too insignificant."

I knew my friend's statement was incorrect, but I didn't know how to answer her scripturally. Within the next few days, as I was reading my Bible, Jesus' words from John 18:37 almost jumped off of the page in front of me: "Everyone that is of the truth heareth my voice."

If that is true—and God's Word is Truth—then *all* believers should be hearing the voice of Jesus. But many are not. Why? I believe there are at least seven reasons why Christians today do not hear from God on a regular (even daily) basis. They are:

1. Lack of faith to believe that hearing from God is for today.

2. Lack of a strong commitment to Jesus Christ as Lord of their life.

3. The presence of unconfessed sin and a "double-standard" lifestyle.

4. Ignorance of the scriptural evidence of the believer's privilege to hear from God personally.

5. Lack of teaching on how to pursue such a listening prayer experience.

6. Fear of being called a "religious fanatic" or "mentally ill."

7. Fear of being open to the "wrong spirits" or being led astray by the enemy.

I would like to help you dispel your fears and doubts. Let's look together at what God's Word has to say about the listening prayer experience.

Commanded To Listen

Let's deal with the first reason many people do not hear from God today: *Lack of faith.* The best way to build faith is by looking to Scripture—"Faith cometh by hearing, and hearing by the word of God" (Romans 10:17).

Mark 9:1-7 records the "mountain top experience" of three of the Lord's disciples. When Jesus took

Peter, James, and John to the top of a mountain, He knew something extraordinary was about to happen. Six days earlier He had told His disciples, "Some of you who are standing here right now will live to see the Kingdom of God arrive in great power!"(verse 1, *TLB*).

For these three disciples, this was the day! Before their very eyes, Jesus' face began to shine with glory and His clothing became dazzling white. Their vocabularies were inadequate to describe what they saw. Then Elijah and Moses appeared and began talking with Jesus.

What happened next? Exactly what might happen today. One of the disciples, Peter, started nervously talking—not really having anything significant to say but compelled to talk.

Even before Peter finished what he was saying, a cloud covered them, and a voice from the cloud said, "*This* is my beloved Son. Listen to *him*" (verse 7, *TLB*).

Sovereignly and supernaturally, God commanded Peter to hush and listen to Jesus. I believe God would like to shout that message to all of us: "*Listen to Jesus.*" But, like Peter, most of us are still talking—because the silence makes us nervous.

God's Spokesman

God commands us to listen to Jesus because Jesus is speaking the words of God. Christ said, "I have not spoken of myself; but the Father which sent me, he gave me a commandment, what I should say, and what I should speak" (John 12:49).

Jesus told His disciples, "I have called you friends [not servants]; for all things that I have heard of my Father I have made known unto you" (John 15:15).

Later, when praying for His disciples, Jesus said, "[Father], I have given unto them the words which thou gavest me; and they have received them" (John 17:8). We see clearly that Jesus told His followers the words that He had heard from God. You may say, That was fine for the people living in Jesus' time, but what about today—how can Jesus still speak to us?

When Jesus told the disciples He was going to leave them and return to His Father in heaven, He said they would not be left without a guide and source of instruction. He said,

> "I will ask the Father and he will give you another Comforter, and he will never leave you. He is the Holy Spirit, the Spirit who leads into all truth. The world at large cannot receive him, for it isn't looking for him and doesn't recognize him. But you do, for he lives with you now and some day shall be in you"—John 14:16-17, *TLB*.

The disciples must have wondered, But who will be the source of the Holy Spirit's messages? Will His guidance and teaching be the same as that of the Father and Jesus? Their doubts and fears were dispelled when Jesus said, "When the Holy Spirit, who is all truth, comes, he shall guide you into all truth, for he will not be presenting his own ideas, but will be passing on to you what he has heard" (John 16:13, *TLB*).

In other words, Jesus said the Holy Spirit would replace Him here on earth as God's spokesman from heaven. And He will speak only God's words. But how?

Jesus, of course, knew exactly how that would be done. In chapter seventeen of John's gospel, Jesus was praying to the Father and said, "I have declared unto them thy name, and *will declare it*" (verse 26, *italics added*). Jesus Himself would tell the Holy Spirit what He wanted His disciples to hear, and the Holy Spirit would *declare it* to them.

How does the Holy Spirit declare God's messages to us? By Scripture, dreams, visions, angels, gifts of knowledge and wisdom, convictions, mental impressions, circumstances, an audible voice, and many other ways. He speaks sentences into our minds that are as clear to the inner ear of the soul as the audible voice is to the outer ear of the physical person.

Jesus declares the words of God to us through the Holy Spirit—even if He has to use an earthquake or a donkey (see Acts 16:26 and Numbers 22:30). But most often His voice comes to us deep in our spirit through the still small voice of God.

In the book, *Hudson Taylor in Early Years, The Growth of a Soul,* Hudson's Taylor's mandate from God is recorded:

> "Never shall I forget," he wrote, "the feel-
> ing that came over me then. Words can

never describe it. I felt I was in the presence of God, entering into covenant with the Almighty. I felt as though I wished to withdraw my promise, but could not. Something seemed to say, 'Your prayer is answered, your conditions are accepted.' And from that time the conviction never left me that I was called to China."

In Mr. Taylor's mother's written recollections, this experience was described this way: "For distinctly, as if a voice had spoken it, the command was given: 'Then go for Me to China.'"

Hudson Taylor's faithful obedience to the voice of the Holy Spirit changed the course of modern missions and sowed seeds that are still being reaped today.

The Shepherd's Voice

When God sent a voice from heaven, Jesus said, "This voice came not because of me, but for your [the disciples] sakes" (John 12:30). The voice being spoken today is also for our sakes, for we are His present-day disciples.

In referring to God's children as sheep and Himself as the Shepherd, Jesus said, "My sheep hear my voice, and I know them, and they follow me." But "a stranger will they not follow, but will flee from him: for they know not the voice of strangers" (John 10:27,5).

If, when we are listening for Jesus to speak, we hear "another voice," we will recognize it as that of a false shepherd and will not be deceived. God's Word is pure truth, and true sheep recognize it as such. Every true child of God is careful to make sure they are hearing only His voice. Their antennas are "up" constantly to make sure they are not getting off track and into something cultish or occultish.

Why do sheep need to hear the Shepherd's voice? It is a well-known fact that sheep are not the most intelligent of animals. They require a shepherd at all times—someone to lead them everywhere they need to go and into everything they need to do. "I am the Lord thy God which teacheth thee to profit, which leadeth thee by the way that thou shouldest go" (Isaiah 48:17).

The psalmist wrote about God's shepherding of Israel: "He led forth his own people like a flock, guiding them safely through the wilderness. He kept them safe, so they were not afraid" (Psalm 78:52-53, *TLB*).

Like the Israelites, we need a shepherd. For this reason, God provided Jesus Christ and the Holy Spirit. As the words of God are told to Jesus and transmitted to us through the Holy Spirit's inaudible, conversational voice inside our mind (or by any of the methods He uses to speak to us) *we hear.* Then our paths become clear and our ways are made profitable—all for the glory of God the Father!

For me, hearing the voice of God is a matter of *faith*. I know God speaks; and I know that when I listen, I hear. Jesus said, "He that hath my commandments and keepeth them . . . I will love him, and will manifest myself to him . . . and my Father will love him, and we will come unto him, and make our abode with Him'' (John 14:21,23).

Jesus *is* manifesting Himself to me, just as He said He would. He *does* abide in my spirit through the Holy Spirit. He tells me many things I need to know about my affairs and those of my family. He gives me guidance, direction, conviction, admonition, revelation, and motivation. I believe Jesus longs to do the same for all those who love Him and follow Him as Shepherd.

The Hungry Sheep Syndrome

The fact that you are reading this book indicates that you are probably truly hungry and thirsty to know God personally. You have a deep longing after God Himself.

You have been ''looking up'' to find God, but you don't feel satisfied in your soul. You know you are seated at the Father's table, but you don't know how to alleviate the hunger pangs and get filled with the manna that satisfies. As a hungry sheep you want to experience the fire that the holy prophets wrote about and the psalmists sang of in their songs. You want to be warmed by the fire of God's personal presence.

Listening prayer is the ideal way for you to begin to satisfy your hungry heart. The first thing to do is to recognize that more of what you are already consuming will not satisfy you.

In the physical realm, we all know that larger amounts of low-nutrient foods will not take away hunger. The more junk foods you eat, the more you want. Although your body is starving for nourishment, consuming larger quantities of low-value foods only heightens the problem. The deep-seated need for missing nutrients has not been met.

The same principle applies in the spiritual realm. We need spiritually dense foods. We can gorge ourselves on Bible study, prayer, Christian fellowship, praise and worship, witnessing, and faithful church attendance, but still lack a missing nutrient. What or *Who* is it?

. The missing part is God Himself. It takes a personal experience and close friendship with God to produce in us the perfect state of spiritual health, regardless of what else we eat or do not eat in the way of spiritual food. Without this personal relationship, we are helpless to digest and assimilate the spiritual diet that will produce the proper results within us. It takes God to satisfy our hungers and thirsts. "Christ in you" is the great secret to perfect spiritual health and successful living.

If Jesus Christ is the same yesterday, today, and forever, then He will fulfill in our lives the words of Isaiah: "And the Lord shall guide thee continually, and satisfy thy soul in drought, and make fat thy bones: and thou shalt be like a watered garden, and like a spring of water, whose waters fail not" (58:11).

Only Jesus can satisfy your hungry and thirsty soul with His sweet presence. He will make your life an overflowing spring spilling over and blessing others.

Harken To His Voice

Have you ever noticed how children learn as they are growing up? How do they understand that they must not cross the street without first looking in both directions? How do they learn *anything* we want them to know? We teach them by repeating the same concepts over and over dozens of times. So it is with you and me, especially in spiritual matters. If we "get it," it will most likely be because we have earnestly sought after it, time and time again.

One day in my quiet time with the Lord, He spoke these words to me. They reveal how desperately Jesus wants to speak to His followers today:

> "My Spirit is pleading with you to be faithful to the listening process. Great ideas filled with truth are ready to be showered upon you, in the name of Jesus and by My exclusive power. Open up your mind, and open up your heart. For the words you receive will be about both physical and spiritual matters, and their two purposes will be made clear as you go along.
>
> "The courtesy of desiring the knowledge of My ways for individual and specific situations is never cancelled out by an insensitive or inattentive God. My business is to shepherd My flock, and that I do with great love and skill beyond reproach.
>
> "Harken to My voice. My desire is to live and move in and through you. Hear Me."

Faith for anything spiritual comes by hearing what the Holy Spirit shows us through His ministry as teacher, counselor, guide, intercessor, etc. And how will we receive faith? By reading His Word and listening to His voice.

CHAPTER FIVE

Discerning The Voice Of God

The work of the Holy Spirit in listening prayer is marked by a balance between the *power* of the Spirit—as demonstrated through making His voice heard—and *holiness* in the life of the believer.

Those who lack personal holiness may hear supernatural messages from supernatural voices, but they will not be from the only true God. Let this be a warning to anyone who wants to savor the flavor without being willing to use the salt!

Not all committed Christians receive guidance through hearing God's voice, but I believe that all who hear His voice in listening prayer *are* committed Christians. These believers have grown to recognize His voice and will not follow another shepherd.

The Good Shepherd "calls his own sheep by name and leads them out. He walks ahead of them; and they follow him, for they recognize his voice. They won't follow a stranger but will run from him, for

they don't recognize his voice" (John 10:3-5, *TLB*).
When true listeners hear from the Lord, no one can
convince us that we have heard another's voice.

Recognizing The Father's Voice

If you are an adult and your father is still living,
it is easy for you to recognize his voice anywhere you
hear it—by phone, over TV, on a cassette tape, or
by shouting from a distance. You wouldn't have
any trouble distinguishing your father's voice and
knowing when you heard it.

The same is true of our heavenly Father's voice.
When you have heard it over and over again, you
learn to recognize it and you cannot be fooled. But
knowing God's voice is a skill we cannot inherit; it
must be developed. Each believer must learn to
recognize God's voice for himself.

When the prophet Samuel was only a young boy,
he became the high priest's helper. One night he was
awakened by a male voice, and he thought it was Eli
calling him. He went to Eli's bedside, but the old
man said he had not called. The boy went back to
sleep, but the same thing happened two more times.
Eli told Samuel that if he heard the voice again to
answer by saying, "Yes, Lord, I'm listening." (See
1 Samuel 3.)

On the fourth call, Samuel recognized God's voice
and told Him he was ready to listen. After that night,
Samuel no longer needed to go to Eli when he heard
a voice calling to him. Samuel learned to discern the
voice of God for himself.

Once we have heard the Father's voice for ourselves, we will not be easily fooled by a counterfeit. One day during a time of listening prayer, I heard something that I immediately knew was not true. I heard, "Test your faith. Give up your work (at the University), and trust Me to support you for awhile." Under the circumstances, nothing about that statement made sense, and my mind said, "That is not from God."

Then the Lord spoke these words to me, "Satan's ideas are always suspect to My child who leans on Me, My Son Jesus, and the Holy Spirit for guidance and sustenance. I will give the order when you are to leave your career, and it will not be you testing your faith. It will be you obeying My voice."

Another time I heard and recorded, "You are trying to get ahead of Me." My mind cut in, and I thought, "That is simply not true." Immediately I heard, "I am pleased to see how quick you are to sense untruth. I am faithful, as you said in your praise this morning. Faithfulness is My very character. You can count on Me to put 'checks' on your messages when they are out of line or in error."

How wonderful to know that God has given us His Holy Spirit to protect us from false spiritual guidance that could bring confusion and doubt.

How can we know for sure we have heard the Holy Spirit giving us God's message? Is it possible to hear another voice and mistake it for God's? Yes, we might hear Satan's voice or that of one of his angels. We could even hear the voice of our own desires. So how can we be sure we have heard from God? Let's look at some tests we can use to discern the voice of God.

The Final Authority

The written *Word of God,* the Bible, is always the final authority to judge what we have heard during listening prayer. God's Word takes precedence over what we feel, hear, think we hear, are impressed by, or over any other sign or leading we receive.

For example, suppose you are a married woman who has permitted yourself to develop affection for another man. You pray about this matter and hear a clear voice say, "Go ahead. You deserve the love you are not receiving from your husband." In this situation you should know immediately that the voice is not God's because His Word repeatedly forbids infidelity in marriage.

If we have heard God's voice, His message will be in perfect alignment with the Word of God. We can be sure that He will not contradict Himself. His Word is absolutely trustworthy and immutable. The Bible says that heaven and earth may pass away but God's words will not. (See Luke 21:33.) If one jot or one tittle of what we have heard contradicts God's Word, we know immediately and definitely that we have *not* heard the voice of the Holy Spirit.

Peace Or Push?

There is another sure way to test the source of what you have heard through listening prayer. God's personal word to you is always accompanied by a deep *inner peace* that comes only from God. Believers learn to recognize this peace from the moment we are born again. The first reward of our prayer of true repentance is a sense of cleanness and well-being—a deep inner peace. Psalm 85:8 says, "I am listening carefully to all the Lord is saying—for He speaks peace to His people, His saints, if they stop their sinning."

On the other hand, when you hear a counterfeit voice or the voice of your own human nature, questions, doubts, and restlessness of spirit always follow. Someone said that Satan pushes, and with his push comes anxiety, frustration, and unsettling thoughts. In contrast, God leads, and with the leading there is an accompanying spirit of peace that cannot be counterfeited.

"The wisdom that comes from heaven is first of all pure and full of quiet gentleness. Then it is peace-loving and courteous" (James 3:17, *TLB*). This verse is the proving ground by which we can judge for ourselves whether or not what we heard was from God. One thing that Satan cannot counterfeit is the peace of God. This inner peace is one of the most accurate tests of divine guidance.

God's messages—all of them—bring a calmness in our spirit and a peace in our hearts that we cannot mistake. Our mind stops flitting from one uncertain thought or fear to another. Our restless spirit settles down to quietness, and our heart is at rest. We can say with David, "I will both lay me down in peace, and sleep" (Psalm 4:8).

Remember, "God is not the author of confusion, but of peace" (1 Corinthians 14:33). The Holy Spirit always speaks with full authority and utters nothing that is not revealed directly from the Father. His instructions are never cloudy or unclear. The Holy Spirit is never confused nor are His words confusing. When we hear from Him, we will be at peace and know exactly what God wants us to do.

God loves us enough to tell it like it is—even when His words are not pleasant or soothing to our flesh. Sometimes God speaks challenging "orders" to us that require a new measure of courage, faith, sacrifice, or even a change in lifestyle. If we obey His instructions or accept His correction, we will always contribute to our spiritual growth and to our ultimate happiness. Although God's words to us may not be exactly what we want to hear, they will still produce only peace and a sense of "rightness" in our spirits.

The Test Of Time

The third way to test whose voice you have heard requires the passage of *time*. Did the message you received come to pass or accomplish what was forecast? This test takes longer to measure, but its results are valid just the same. There is one problem with this test that many Christians sometimes fail to recognize—*God's sense of timing is different from man's.* Let me illustrate this truth from Scripture.

Throughout the ages, God has required His children to wait on His timing for the fulfillment of His promises. Caleb was promised a piece of the promised land because he believed God would grant the children of Israel victory. He waited *forty-five years* for God to fulfill this promise. Nonetheless, God was faithful, and Caleb entered the land of Canaan—when the time was right.

At the age of forty, Moses felt the call of God on his life to see his people delivered. And they were— *forty years later*—when Moses was eighty years old!

Noah was told by God to build an ark, but He didn't tell him it would take *one hundred and twenty years* to complete the project. Yet, during all that time, Noah did not lose confidence in God.

Joseph, due to no sin of his own, was held for *fifteen* years in slavery in Egypt—two years of that time in prison—before God used him in the ministry to which he had been called.

David, Abraham and Sarah, Paul, Daniel, and even Jesus were given promises and messages from God that were not fulfilled immediately. Nonetheless, each one "in God's own time" had their Word from the Lord fulfilled to perfection. And since God is the same yesterday, today, and forever, He is still fulfilling His Word in the lives of today's saints.

In her book, *My God Will Supply*, Dede Robertson, the wife of Pat Robertson, tells how the Lord guided them at a turning point in their lives. Take special note of the tests Pat and Dede used to discern the voice of God.

Before we left Lexington, a letter came to Pat's mother from an old family friend named George Lauderdale who lived in the Tidewater area of the state. In the postscript (it's amazing how many of life's big events come in a P.S.) George mentioned that there was a television station for sale in Portsmouth, Virginia. George wondered if Pat would be interested in claiming Channel 27 for the Lord?

We chuckled at the thought. The whole episode was refreshing. It felt good to laugh. My spirits lifted. "Claiming a station for the Lord; he means buying it, doesn't he, Pat?"

"Yes, I would say so, Dede."

"And after the great tag sale we don't have one hundred dollars to our name!" I said, still amused.

Pat was laughing, too.

"We certainly don't know anything about running a television station," he added.

"We don't even own a television set," Tim said, a little bitterly.

We were still . . . wondering where we were supposed to go when something strange happened to me. I was visiting friends from the seminary. Someone asked me, "Dede, do you and Pat know yet what your work is going to be?"

"Yes," I answered, just as quick as that. "The Lord is sending Pat to Virginia to buy a television station."

It was something I just knew. There was no explaining it.

The Lord was leading us with increasing clarity now. That same night in our bedroom while Pat and I were praying in tongues I thought I heard the Lord urging me to read 1 Chronicles 10:12. I was about to tell Pat when he spoke first.

"Dede," Pat said, "I'm almost certain the Lord is asking me to fast and pray for a week. Is he saying anything to you?"

"Well, yes. I keep hearing the words '1 Chronicles 10:12.' "

"Do you know what they say?"

"No I don't, Pat." I was already thumbing through my Bible. These words jumped out at me. " . . . and they fasted seven days."

Twice in succession this mysterious phenomenon had happened to us, and if it never happened again it didn't matter. The Lord was giving us clear, step-by-step directions when we needed them most. . . .

The very next morning Pat went into the adventure of staying in our drafty, dark, old church for seven days.

After the first two days a peace settled over me. The children and I went about our daily routines. . . .

At last, the seventh day came and . . . I heard Pat's approaching footsteps. He pulled open the heavy door. The man who stood facing me was radiant! He needed a shave; and his hair was mussed and his clothes were rumpled, but there was a set to his shoulders and a light in his eyes that told me more clearly than words that here was a person who had talked with God.

"Dede, I've got the answer," Pat said, a grin suggesting itself around his luminous eyes. "Has He spoken to you, too?"

"Yes," I said, "and I think we have the same message."

"We're going to Virginia," Pat said, standing there holding my hands and grinning at me.

"I know," I said.

We both began to laugh and dance in a circle.

Before taking any action, Pat and Dede tested the guidance they had received. They confirmed it from God's Word and waited until they had the peace of God in their hearts. Finally, the test of time has proven that Pat and Dede Robertson were directly guided by the Lord. As you probably know, Pat Robertson went to Virginia Beach, purchased a small television station, and began the *700 Club*, which later grew to become the worldwide ministry of the Christian Broadcasting Network.

Making Sure

If you think God has spoken to you, yet doubt remains in your mind, I have a method that can help you determine whose voice you have heard. If you can respond to the following statements affirmatively, then rest assured that God is speaking to you.

1. What I heard helps me to respect (fear) the Lord and to depart from evil. (See Job 28:28.)

2. The message increases my faith in or my knowledge and understanding of Scripture. (See Proverbs 4:7.)

3. The actions that will result from following this will be full of spiritual fruits: purity, peace, gentleness, mercy, courtesy, good deeds, sincerity, and without hypocrisy. (See James 3:17.)

4. What I heard strengthens me "with all might" so that I can keep going no matter what happens. (See Colossians 1:11.)

5. It causes me to experience joyfulness and thanksgiving to the Father. (See Colossians 1:12.)

If you can answer "yes" to each of these questions, then you can rest assured that the direction or word you have received is from God and will bring blessing to you and everyone involved. If, however, you are still in doubt, I advise you to do as Pat Robertson did and take some time to fast and pray before you venture forth—especially if you are making a decision that will dramatically affect your life and future.

God in His wisdom has provided ways for us to test whether or not we have truly heard His voice.

Don't rush off in your pride or presumption with a word that may be from "another shepherd." Waiting and testing will help you avoid making a mistake. Remember, God is never in a hurry.

CHAPTER SIX

Personal Guidance In Difficult Times

My main purpose in writing this book is to share what I have learned about listening prayer—to tell you that I tried it and it worked! I am totally convinced that God's plan from the beginning was to give personal guidance to each of His children. "The God of our fathers hath chosen thee, that thou shouldest know his will, and see that Just One, and shouldest *hear the voice of his mouth*" (Acts 22:14, *italics added*).

From Genesis 1 to Revelation 21, I can find nothing to the contrary. We are made to have a conversational relationship with God, for a *divine* purpose. "Out of heaven he made thee to hear his voice, that he might instruct thee" (Deuteronomy 4:36).

Someone recently said that 95 percent of what we need to know from God about how to live can be found by searching the scriptures. That means 5 percent of our decisions require divine guidance of a specific and personal nature. I feel that more than 5 percent of my problems need the Holy Spirit's personal attention—maybe 10-15 percent.

At one point in my life I had to seek God's help continuously for specific guidance concerning my relationship with my son and daughter. Let me share with you how God graciously worked in several situations in our lives.

Unacceptable Behavior

In 1978 our son, who was then twenty-eight, was living as a hippie in New York City, having "dropped-out-of-the-system." Although our twenty-five-year-old daughter was a nurse, she had been greatly influenced by her brother's rebellious philosophy and had adopted his radical lifestyle in many ways.

That summer my husband Don and I were returning from vacation in Florida. As we approached the town where our daughter was working, we telephoned. Her brother was visiting her at the time, so we asked if we could take them to lunch.

We arrived as planned, and they were ready for us. Unfortunately, we were not ready for them! Stephen was dressed in dirty coveralls, fishing boots, and an army-surplus jacket full of holes and covered with spots of paint. His braided hair hung twelve inches below shoulder length, and he wore a bandana around his forehead. Strong body odor mixed with his alcohol breath created a rather nauseating smell—especially over lunch.

Susan was a bit better. She was dressed to go directly from lunch to the hospital where she was working. In my opinion, however, her long, stringy hair needed a shampoo, and her nurses' shoes were too dirty to meet my standards. Her uniform was clean enough but far from wrinkle-free. She certainly didn't match my image of a Florence Nightingale—especially when her attitude toward us was far from loving and compassionate.

One glance at them made me ask myself a question: "Will the maitre d' at the restaurant where they want to go be willing to seat us?" I truly was not sure.

During the meal, conversation was stifled at every attempt made, and we could find no common ground for discussion. The entire visit was a fiasco and a truly devastating experience for me.

A Word From God

After we left Stephen and Susan and started toward home, I had a knot in my throat too large to be swallowed and too cemented in place to be coughed up. I began to cry: "Lord, where are You? How much more will You require us to take? What in the world are You hoping to accomplish through all of this?"

Then the Lord spoke clearly. He said, "Mary Ruth, I am waiting for *you* to show My kind of love. My love never fails, never excludes, and never limits."

I got the message and saw immediately that my love was saying, "If you, Stephen, would just get that hair cut, replace those crazy clothes with a grey flannel suit, buy a pair of Florsheim wing-tips instead of those rubber boots, etc. . . . *Then* I would do so and so to get you straightened out! My list of "if you would's" for Susan were equally as easy to recite.

For the next one hundred miles, I prayed, cried, and thought—and became more depressed than I had ever been in my life. When we got home, I was so overcome that I did not have the strength to unpack my clothes. Instead, I went to my newly established prayer closet and asked the Father if He had a word for me. He did. I wrote it down, but somehow it did nothing for me. So I had a bath and went to bed three hours before my regular bedtime.

The next morning I got up early, went to my prayer closet and reread the message I had received the night before. This time my faith was renewed. Somehow I knew that God was in charge of my children, and my task was to keep believing they would be changed. Here is what the Lord told me:

> "Your children are not your children. They belong to Me, and I am tending to their needs and caring for their passions. They are learning to hear My calling and are coming close to hearing My promptings. They both love Me, but they are very immature.
>
> "You slow them down by your enthusiasm and your desire to see them become new creatures. Listen for Me to guide you, and stop being headstrong and showing a lack of understanding of their problems.

"Trust Me and be patient. Someday you will be proud of them for they will love Me with their whole hearts, and their behavior will shape up and fall in line. They have been very stubborn, but those days are about over. They are beginning to see the error of their ways. They know they have some changing to do, and they are becoming pliable in My hands. Continue to love them not only for what they are but for what they are becoming.

"I am waiting for you to show My kind of patience. Start resting entirely in My peace. Who can care for them better than I? A greater love than I have for them is impossible, for my love gives all and asks nothing in return. That is why My love finally melts stony hearts and molds young people into men and women of real character.

"Your dreams are being realized. Be steadfast and unmovable in your faith in them and toward Me. In the Name of Jesus, great things are happening tonight. Both children are thinking about what you shared with them today. Lay your burden down and rest. In time your faithfulness to Me will be blessed."

While I probably failed to "rest" to the extent that the Lord would have desired, I did experience immediate relief from my depression. New hope was born in my heart as I read the message over and over—for weeks!

You may be struggling through a similar situation with your children. But take heart. If you are faithful to pray for them, God will be faithful to do the impossible. In the meantime, *rest* and let Him do all the work.

The Family Reunion

Six months after our luncheon meeting with Stephen and Susan, my sister invited all of us to a family reunion. When I thought about the impression my children would make on my very proper and elite family, I became extremely anxious. But I decided to face the situation with God's help and hope for the best.

My sister's home, which in itself is a showplace, was decorated throughout with cut flowers. The country club catered an elegantly served meal, and everything was "first class." It was a beautiful day, perfect for a pleasant family gathering— except for one thing: my children.

Susan made an effort to look nice by not wearing the shabby blue jeans she habitually wore when not in uniform, but her "compromise" was almost as bad. She also continued to flaunt her long tumbledown hairstyle. Stephen had on a pair of totally worn-out blue jeans and a wild-looking top. Both children screamed "rebellion" without opening their mouths.

My luncheon table for four included a sister-in-law, my aunt, and my mother. Just as we sat down, Mother straightened up and said with fury in her voice, "Well, Mary Ruth, it's a good thing those two of yours aren't *my* kids; I'd straighten them out!"

My humiliation already had me ready to burst into tears at any moment, but I answered as calmly as possible, "Well, Mother, if I thought you could do that, I would certainly be glad to turn them over to you."

At that, my aunt got involved and patted Mother on the arm, trying to calm her emotions and change the subject to more pleasant topics. It worked, and we went on with our delicious lunch.

On the way home, I prayed and asked God how much longer I had to wait to see my children change and how much more He was going to require Don and me to endure before that time. Then it happened!

As clearly as I ever heard anyone speak to me, the Holy Spirit said, "Mary Ruth, if you had your way, your children would both have doctorates and would be climbing the ladder of success the world's way. Then you would look at them so proudly and tell everyone, 'See what *I* did *all by myself.*' But when I get them straightened out and you see how I use them for Kingdom purposes, you will be able to say, 'Don't give me *any* of the credit; everything you see them accomplishing is because of what the Lord did for them. I didn't have anything to do with it—nothing at all!'"

That message had the comparable effect of a tranquilizer, and it lasted for months—even years.

Just What I Needed To Hear

The weekend before Thanksgiving in 1979, Susan came to visit dressed in clothes that, to me, were totally unacceptable. We exchanged a few words about her 1920s moth-eaten, mink-dyed muskrat coat with strips of rotted lining hanging down like fringe on a drapery. There was no screaming or fighting or anything like that. I just calmly expressed my disapproval, and Susan replied with, "I don't give a d . . . how you feel about it."

When she returned home, Susan wrote me a six-page letter saying she would never set foot in our house again. She then phoned to say she would be coming the next weekend so we could "have it out." She said I could read the whole letter then and tell her my responses—and our case would be forever settled! I was devastated even to think that such an unpleasant confrontation might take place within the walls of our peaceful home.

What did I do? I went to my prayer closet and asked God how to handle this case. It was nine o'clock in the morning, November 29, Thanksgiving Day. At 11:45 a.m. Don knocked on my prayer closet door and reminded me that we were due at friends' for dinner at 12:30 p.m. Although I had been listening to hear God's voice for nearly three hours without a break, I had heard nothing.

All during dinner and afterwards, while watching a slide show of our friends' latest trip abroad, I prayed in the spirit and listened with my heart for God to speak. No answer yet.

Upon returning home after dinner, I immediately went back to my prayer closet. I sought the Lord again, praising Him for an answer and asking for a word from Him before bedtime. I needed to hear within two days. Susan was coming home on Saturday.

At 9:00 p.m., I still had not heard one word, although I had listened for about ten hours. My hip bones actually hurt from long hours of sitting on a rather hard surface. Despite the fact that I had told the Lord at about 6:30 p.m., "I plan to sit here until you answer me," I gave up. Just as I raised up to leave my closet, He said, "Go upstairs, have a bath, get your Bible, and get in bed." I obeyed exactly.

Immediately upon getting in bed, the Lord said, "Open your Bible, and begin to read." I did, and the pages fell open to Matthew 9:18: "My little daughter has just died, but you can bring her back to life again if you will only come and touch her" (*TLB*). I knew this verse referred to my daughter's spiritual condition at the present time. Until she was sixteen years old, Susan had been a model child by any mother's standard. Now I knew God *could* bring her back to life again.

Then my eyes fell on a tract that had been placed on that page in my Bible. The title was "The New Birth." The Lord said, "The only hope for Susan to change her mode of dress and lifestyle is to be brought to new life spiritually. *Nothing* you can say will do it. Jesus must change her mind and her will. She must totally dedicate herself to Him."

I looked down at my Bible a third time, and my eyes fell on the words, "Because of your faith it will happen" (Matthew 9:29, *TLB*). Of course, I knew that was true; I had always believed for the total salvation of my children.

Turning to another chapter in the Bible, I read, "There can be no joy for me until He acts." And that was it! I had my answer. I knew that nothing I could say or do would change the situation. God had to act, and when He did, the perfect answer for both of us—for all of us—would be found.

My conclusion? Listening prayer is not learned in a classroom but in a prayer closet, and this "lesson" lasted exactly ten hours. What a small price to pay for the answer to a complex and difficult problem. I could have spent many months—and many dollars—counseling with a "professional" without ever receiving a "sure word of Truth." But The Counselor went straight to the heart of the matter and told me just what I needed to hear.

The Confrontation

When Susan came for the Saturday visit, the scene was both pathetic and hilarious. Instead of her usual drooped-shoulders posture, Susan's head was held high. Her backbone was so straight she looked like someone had rammed a steel poker through her spinal column.

Don and I met her at the door. Brushing past us with the grace of a movie star, she said, "Well, Daddy, do you want to be in on this or not?"

Poor Don. "My first preference, Susan," he replied, "is for you and your mother to talk. I'll go to my room. If you want me to come, just let me know." Susan and I went into the living room alone.

She got the letter out of her purse and handed it to me with the same gusto that a banker might thrust a six-figure overdue note at one of his customers. I took it, sat down, and tore the envelope open.

The first page was so acidic that I folded it back up, placed it in the envelope, handed it to Susan, and said, "Honey, since nothing you have said on page one is true from my point of view, and since it is written with bitterness in every word, I think I would rather not read the rest of the letter. After all, I have the answer to our problem."

In typical soap opera style, she replied, "Oh, you *do*, do you? Well, what is it?"

I said, "I don't think you would be interested because it is spiritual in nature."

"Oh, yes I would," she said. "Tell me."

I went to my prayer closet, got my journal, turned to the page for Thanksgiving Day and began to read. By the time I had finished, she had slumped down on the sofa as if an unseen angel had pulled the rod out of her spine. She stared at me for quite a long time as both of us sat in silence. Then, with a very different tone to her voice, she said, "Mother, I have to buy a pair of nurses shoes while I'm here. Would you like to go uptown with me?"

We went shopping and actually had a good time. Since then we have never had a confrontation like the one that day. In fact, about one year later, Don and I took Susan to lunch. About half-through the meal she said, "Mother and Daddy, I want to tell you that I have taken a one-hundred-and-eighty-degree turn in my attitude. Before, I did not want to be one bit like Mother, but I now want to be exactly like her." We could hardly believe our ears, but we are still praising the Lord for this victory.

Two years later, Susan confessed her sins and accepted Jesus Christ as her Savior—without the help of anyone but the Holy Spirit. About the same time, Stephen phoned to say he had recommitted his life to Jesus, trusting Him as Savior and Lord. At the time of this writing, I can truthfully and humbly say I am very proud of both of my children. They have become our dearest friends and co-laborers with us in our ministry.

A Vision Of Romance

Soon after my daughter Susan became a Christian, she and her girlfriend, Barbara, attended a Full Gospel Businessmen's dinner. During the preliminaries, Susan said to Barbara, "Look at the fourth man to the right of the podium at the head of the table. He is my idea of an ideal-looking man for a husband." As girls will do, they continued to giggle and joke about the possibility of marrying this handsome young man.

The president of the Fellowship brought the meeting to order and introduced a local medical doctor—the fourth man from the right of the podium! With rapt attention, the girls listened as he gave a few words of personal testimony before introducing the guest speaker for the evening. Susan and Barbara, both relatively new Christians, were quite impressed by this special doctor.

After the meeting ended, the doctor and the girls ended up using the same exit, arriving at the door at exactly the same time. In fact, Susan held the door for the doctor and an older couple whom she suspected (correctly, she later learned) were his parents.

Susan called long distance to give me an account of this event, and two days later I had a vision. I saw a doctor walking toward me down a hospital corridor as he seriously studied the charts on his clipboard. He came so close to me that I could give a detailed description of his features. When the vision left, I asked the Lord, "What's that all about?"

I heard, "Susan will marry a medical doctor who is a very serious-minded and caring person." I later shared this vision with Susan, telling her every detail.

Two weeks passed, and I had another vision almost exactly like the first. This time the same doctor, still studying the chart on his clipboard, came to the end of the hallway where I was standing. Then he turned and went down the stairway exit.

The Lord asked, "Where does a doctor go when he walks away from the nurses station to the end of the corridor?"

I said, "I don't know, Lord."

He said, "Most likely he goes down the stairs to an office and then home."

"Maybe he'll meet her on his way home!" I thought. "And soon!"

Twenty-three days later, at another Full Gospel Businessmen's dinner, Susan and Dr. David Darbro met. The details are still exciting to me but probably too lengthy to be included here. In any event, they were married thirteen months later.

I marvel at the goodness and faithfulness of our great God. Every word He gave me concerning my children has come to pass. His personal guidance during the difficult times enabled me to act with wisdom that I would not have had otherwise. And God will do the same for you if you will take the time to seek His direction for every relationship and every need in your life.

CHAPTER SEVEN

Steps Ordered By The Lord

God wants to be involved in every detail of our lives. As a loving heavenly Father, He delights in leading us and ordering each step we take. The psalmist was right when he wrote, "The steps of a good man are ordered by the Lord: and he delighteth in his way" (Psalm 37:23). All God asks is that we admit that we need His help: "In all thy ways acknowledge him, and he shall direct thy paths" (Proverbs 3:6).

In my prayer closet, I seek God's direction for my life, asking Him to "order my steps." I have learned that He can orchestrate and master my destiny much better than I can. When I acknowledge my need for His direction, He is always faithful to show me the perfect path to take.

The Threads Of Obedience

In the summer of 1978, we received a wedding invitation from my husband's niece in Connecticut.

Don and I did not discuss going until it was time to make plane reservations. When Don brought the subject up, I told him that for some reason I didn't believe I was to go. I felt that he was but I wasn't. This shocked him. In fact, he was visibly upset. We had always gone to affairs like this together.

I asked Don if he would be willing to seek the Lord for a definite answer as to what we were to do. I, too, agreed to pray for God's direction. In my prayer closet that morning, I asked the Lord what we should do. This is the message that I recorded in my journal:

> "It is My will for Don to carry through with his plans to go to Connecticut, and it is My will for you to remain here alone. Rest in My peace and comfort, both of you. I can see the whole design clearly. In the end you will see it, too.
>
> "The threads you both must weave into the picture cannot be done by forsaking these arrangements. Please hear Me and follow through. Don needs to share his faith with his family, and they can be helped by having him alone for a few days. I will bless you for seeking knowledge about this trip."

When Don and I met for lunch, he said, "Well, I have my answer about going to Connecticut."

I said, "Great, so do I. What is your answer?"

He said, "I was reading Matthew 22:4 this morning, and the words 'come unto the marriage' seemed to speak directly to me and the situation—so I think I am supposed to go."

After I read him my message, both of us knew we had heard from the Lord. And we knew we had to obey. The events that happened as a result of our obedience were exciting and far beyond our greatest expectations.

Timely Encounters

Less than three hours after I took Don to the airport for his flight to Connecticut, I had a long-distance telephone call from a colleague of mine in another state. With desperation in her voice, she said, "Mary Ruth, this is Elizabeth. I am unexpectedly in the hospital this morning, facing emergency surgery. Two days from now, I am scheduled to give the key address at a meeting of professionals in Arizona. I heard that you recently gave an excellent speech in Dallas. Could you possibly go to Flagstaff in my place and speak to this group?" I accepted her invitation and made plans to go to Arizona.

The first miracle of the trip took place in the airport terminal, where I met two African students who knew me from my work with the Foreign Student Association on campus. They had a friend named Lucas with them who was also from their home country of Kenya.

On the plane I sat next to Lucas. Soon after take-off, I asked him about his religious beliefs. We exchanged ideas for the whole flight, and just before landing at our destination he leaned over and asked, "If a person wanted to accept Jesus as their Savior, how would they do it?"

I excitedly replied, "You've asked the right person!" And I led him through the sinner's prayer. By the radiant look on his face, I knew he had experienced a release of guilt and received the blessing of God's peace in his heart.

During the ten minutes I was rushing to a far corner of the terminal to catch my connecting flight, Lucas and I talked about the essentials of Christianity—daily Bible reading, prayer, witnessing, tithing, water baptism, fellowship with other Christians, and so forth. He gave me his home address, and I promised to pray for him and send him a *Living Bible*. We said good-bye and went our separate ways.

Reaping The Rewards

When I got off the plane in Phoenix, a woman was holding a plaque with my name written on it. I was a bit frightened and wondered what this could mean. She explained that my flight to Flagstaff (the last of the day) had been cancelled. The airline was having the Greyhound bus held so I could be a passenger on it—the last one leaving that day. She gave me a refund of forty-three dollars, paid my taxi fare to the bus station, and bid me good-bye.

The speech went well, and the honorarium was extraordinarily generous. In addition, the view from my hotel window was breath-taking. I only wished that Don could have been there with me to help fill up that king-sized bed!

On the trip home, I had an hour layover in St. Louis. While I waited, a soldier sat down beside me and began to rip open a package. It was a *Living Bible*. I asked him where he got it, and he said, "At that newsstand over there. They have one more left."

Using some of the money from my refunded plane ticket, I bought a Bible for Lucas. While waiting for my plane, I underlined several salvation verses and some "jewels" in the Psalms. Two years later, I received a letter from Kenya. Lucas wrote telling me that he was enjoying being a Christian and that his "most prized possession in this world is the Bible you sent me. I love it!"

Yes, Don and I had heard God correctly. My husband was supposed to go to Connecticut, where he had a wonderful few days with his family, and I was supposed to go to Arizona. From the beginning, God could clearly see the whole design and the beautiful threads He wanted us to weave into this portion of our lives.

The Power To Obey

Although most of us *want* to do God's will, we are incapable of obeying Him in our own strength. That's why God provided the Holy Spirit. When the Holy Spirit is living within us, we have the power to obey and do the will of our Father in heaven.

If you have not sought the baptism of the Holy Spirit, do it now. Only then, I believe, can you fulfill this command from God: "Ye shall walk after the Lord your God, and fear him, and keep his commandments, and *obey his voice,* and ye shall serve him, and cleave unto him" (Deuteronomy 13:4, *italics added*).

What a challenge to all believers—walk with Him, respect Him, keep His statutes, and obey His voice. Before we can obey His voice, however, we must first learn to hear His voice. Then we can serve Him and cleave to Him.

Over the years, the Holy Spirit has helped me to obey God—even when He has changed my course and led me down an unfamiliar path.

Set On A New Course

While attending the Full Gospel Businessmen's Fellowship International annual meeting, I was listening to Kenneth Copeland give his testimony. The content of his message and his humorous method of presenting it captivated my attention.

Suddenly I heard a man whisper in my ear, "I'm going to use you again in nutrition." I jerked my head in the direction of the voice, but no one was there. I had an aisle seat, and no one was sitting beside me. When I glanced behind me, one row back, a women and her three small children looked at me as if to say, "What's wrong with you, lady?"

I knew, from past experience, that the voice I had heard must be God's. So I got an envelope out of my purse and wrote down the sentence He had spoken to me. Although I had a master's degree in Foods and Nutrition, it had been many years since I had worked and taught as a nutritionist.

That same afternoon I was listening to Hilton Sutton speak on the second coming of Christ. Having never heard a sermon on that subject, I found the topic fascinating. In addition, the lecturer's vast knowledge kept me focused on his every word.

Although my mind was totally preoccupied, a second message came to me just as clearly as the first. The Lord said, "I want you to ask American Christians to deny themselves unneeded calories, save the money the calories would have cost, and give it to Great Commission projects and programs in these last days." I knew it was the same voice, so I wrote down the message.

The next afternoon Hilton Sutton spoke again, and I was furiously taking notes on his eschatological message. Then for the third time I heard the same voice say to me, "Put that in the form of an experiment. See if you can motivate Christians to deny themselves unneeded calories."

After that weekend, I did two computer searches to see if such a study had already been done. It hadn't. I designed and completed the study, using twenty-five Christians. In four weeks they denied themselves nearly one-half million calories, lost an aggregate of eighty-seven pounds, and saved $599.96.

The Lord showed me how easily we could raise millions of dollars for Christian endeavors. We could even greatly improve our own health in the process.

By decreasing the incidence of diabetes, heart trouble, high blood pressure, gallstones, kidney stones, cancer, and many other degenerative diseases among Christians, God would be greatly glorified.

Nutrition With A Mission

From that weekend to this present day, God has continued to speak about this new work. He even gave me the name for it: *Nutrition With A Mission*. What is this mission? Fulfilling the Great Commission. Matthew 4:4 in *The Living Bible* is our key verse: "Obedience to every word of God is what we need" to feed our souls. Obedience to every word in the Bible that relates to food would solve our health problems. I knew that then, and I am more sure of it now.

On the Monday after the Full Gospel Businessmen's Convention, as I was praying in my office at noon, I had a vision—one of the first the Lord ever gave me. Clear, clean patches of the carpet on my office floor appeared in rectangular shapes. Each piece lay parallel to the next, with larger patches first, and then smaller and smaller ones until in the far distance the smallest piece was very tiny. I asked the Father the meaning of the vision. He said, "You will have very clear guidance for developing the nutrition project from the very first until it is fully accomplished—as I want it to be."

It is now several years later, and His word has been fulfilled to perfection since that time. Anyone who knows the details of what has happened to me since

February 1978 would agree that I have had clear guidance. Two books, two teaching booklets, many lectures, dozens of seminars, and many television appearances—all of these have been brought miraculously into existence according to the Father's design. To God be the glory for the things He has done!

Hoofs Of Brass

Not long after this vision, as I was praying one day, I heard the Lord clearly say, "Read Micah 4:13 and accept it as a verse for your ministry." I turned to Micah and excitedly read these words: "Rise, thresh, O daughter of Zion; I will give you horns of iron and hoofs of brass and you will trample to pieces many people, and you will give their wealth as offerings to the Lord, the Lord of all the earth" (*TLB*).

Naturally, I had to think about the meaning of that verse. As I meditated on it, God began to give me understanding. It meant that I would rise and begin to work very hard to get prepared for a new work in nutrition. As I did, God would give me strength in my mind (iron horns) and strength for travel (hoofs of brass). My lectures, given to me under the inspiration of the Holy Spirit, would prick the consciences (cut into pieces) of many people. Then they would go along with God's plan of denying themselves unneeded calories and giving that money to Great Commission programs and projects. I am still excited as I think about this blessing coming to pass.

Two months later, in a listening prayer session, the Lord said, "I will reveal knowledge to you. New knowledge. You will bring glory to My name in many places both large and small. Your ministry will be worldwide. If you remain yielded to My Spirit, I will use you mightily. Make haste with My work. Trust Me to show you where to work. I will reveal it."

There is not space for me to tell you how all of this has been or is being fulfilled, but it is. I stand amazed as I watch God fulfill His promises in His perfect timing—never early and never late!

Marching Orders

One morning in 1978 as I was sitting in a meeting with a group of dietitians in Chicago, I heard the Lord say, "I want you to write a nutrition book for me. Write it from the spiritual point of view." I answered: "Fine, Lord. Show me *how* and show me *when*."

Two months later I was in my prayer closet when God began to speak. After two sentences I realized that He was giving me material for His book through me. The first message was 700 words, including the title, *Nutrition for Christians*. Eight days later He gave me 1700 words; by the end of two weeks I had 7300 words ready to print. It was beautiful!

Then God said to me one morning, "Maintain your interest in writing. I will work closely with you at all times. I want you to succeed for, after all, this is My work and they are My children that you will be helping. Rest in My peace. Don't take back the burden of doing things on your own anymore.

Keep remembering, none of this is from you. I am simply using you as an instrument to carry out My special work with Christians, especially those who are overweight or obese."

Early in the new year, 1979, the Lord asked me, "Is it not clearer all the time, Mary Ruth, that your full-time administrative work is not compatible with full-time work for the Kingdom? Be ready to switch at a moment's notice."

Not until May 17, 1979, however, did I know for sure that God wanted me to retire from my work as Dean of the School of Home Economics at Eastern Illinois University. The Lord said, "You need to free yourself from your present job as Dean. Sometime soon I will permit you to be in an environment where you can flourish for Me. Get free-wheeling—both you and Don." Now my husband and I had definite orders. Of course we obeyed them—but not without some fear and trembling on my part.

A Joyful Celebration

The day I heard the Lord tell me it was time to retire I went into an emotional quandary—a state somewhere between elated and fearful. Looking toward a future without a ten to fourteen hour away-from-home job made me wonder how I would fill my time and if I would be happy.

I went to my prayer closet to talk to God about how I felt and asked Him to give me an assurance from the scriptures that I had heard Him correctly.

I heard, "Turn to Nehemiah chapter eight and begin reading with verse nine." I read:

> "Don't cry on such a day as this! For today is a sacred day before the Lord your God—it is a time to celebrate with a hearty meal, and to send presents to those in need, for the joy of the Lord is your strength. You must not be dejected and sad! . . . " So the people went away to eat a festive meal and to send presents; it was a time of great and joyful celebration because they could hear and understand God's words—Nehemiah 8:9-12, *TLB*.

As soon as I read those words, I knew I had heard God correctly. Immediately, I began to make retirement plans.

That same day we actually did have a festive meal and a joyful celebration. I had invited Yen and Jessica, two foreign students from Taiwan, to dinner because they were going to be leaving the university soon. After dinner, we went into the living room to talk about spiritual things. It was beautiful to see how they had grown in the Lord since their salvation experiences only seven months before.

Just before they left for the evening, Yen said, "I want to be a Christian like you. Maybe in forty years I will be. You have taught me how to grow, and I am going to grow even faster now that I know what to do."

God's word to me from Nehemiah was fulfilled perfectly. That day *was* a time of joyful celebration as we rejoiced together in all God had done for them—and for me.

One Step At A Time

As I look back over my life—and especially over the last few years since I have learned to hear God's voice—I can see that God was truly ordering my steps. And He will do the same for you—one step at a time.

> Trust in the Lord with all thine heart; and lean not unto thine own understanding. In all thy ways acknowledge him, and he shall direct thy paths. . . . Then shalt thou walk in thy way safely, and thy foot shall not stumble. . . . For the Lord shall be thy confidence, and shall keep thy foot from being taken—Proverbs 3:5-6,23,26.

God will order your steps as you ask for His direction at each bend in the path and at each crossroad you come to. When you turn to the right or the left, you will hear a voice behind you saying, "This is the way, walk ye in it" (Isaiah 30:21).

CHAPTER EIGHT

The Spirit Of Wisdom

In his letter to the Christians at Ephesus, the apostle Paul mentioned that they had received the Holy Spirit after they had believed in the Lord Jesus Christ. Paul told them he was now praying that the Father would give them "the spirit of wisdom and revelation in the knowledge of him," in order that "the eyes of their understanding" might be enlightened and that they might know "what is the hope of his calling, and . . . the riches of the glory of his inheritance" (Ephesians 1:17,18).

Remember that Paul had stated in the previous verse that these believers had already received the Holy Spirit. So the "spirit of wisdom" that he is asking to be given them must be something "extra"— a special gift from the Holy Spirit.

One thing we know about Paul, the "Hebrew of the Hebrews," is that he knew his Old Testament. The spirit of wisdom he prayed would be given to the Ephesian believers was the same spirit of wisdom

God gave certain Old Testament saints, like Moses, Bezaleel, Solomon, and the promised Messiah.

The first mention of this "spirit of wisdom" gift occurred when the Lord instituted the Levitical priesthood and commanded Moses to ordain Aaron and make him "holy garments . . . for glory and beauty." Moses was to choose those who were skilled in certain areas to do this work, but God said, "I have filled [them] with the *spirit of wisdom*, to make Aaron's garments" (Exodus 28:2-3, *italics added*).

The special gift of wisdom was given to increase the skill of these artisans and help them use their talents for God's glory. If you read the story, you will find that God gave them specific instructions for performing a wide range of tasks, including engraving, embroidery, and the art of making fine jewelry.

During the construction of the tabernacle, craftsmen of every kind were needed to complete the beautiful dwelling for the Lord. God promised, by the spirit of wisdom, to give know-how and expertise to them all. (See Exodus chapters 35-39.) The spirit of wisdom was given to everyone whose heart was stirred by God's Spirit to prepare gifts for the tabernacle project and to those who felt called to do the actual work—including any women who wanted to help.

God gave Solomon the spirit of wisdom, and the Bible says, "He was the author of 3,000 proverbs and wrote 1,005 songs. He was a great naturalist, with interest in animals, birds, snakes, fish, and trees. . . . And kings from many lands sent their ambassadors to him for his advice" (1 Kings 4:32-34, *TLB*). This is an impressive list covering a wide range of subjects.

Whatever your interests or talents, God can give you knowledge and wisdom concerning them—if you ask Him. God has a work to do through each of us. Shouldn't we, then, expect that the same Lord who gave wisdom to Solomon and showed the Israelites how to effect His plan in perfect detail will instruct *us* in our daily work and lives? I believe we can and should expect God to do the same for us today.

Divine Dictation

During the writing of my first book, I came to a point where I could go no further. I was working, thinking, and doing my best, but I simply could not find a way to bring a host of ideas into a circumspect whole.

One evening as I was struggling to write, I decided to go to my prayer closet. The time was 7:00 p.m. I said, "Lord, I have only four hours to spend working on this book tonight. What do You want me to do?" I listened without hearing anything. I opened the door to read my watch, and it was 7:15 p.m. After closing the door, I said, "Lord, please don't keep me waiting. I want to do Your work Your way, and I don't know how. I need Your help. Please help me!"

Just then I heard the Lord say, "Get the last chapter where you were working and continue to write." I did that. I re-read the last few paragraphs and started to work. I would write a few sentences and mark them out; write a few more and mark half of them out! I was very frustrated, to say the least.

I looked at my watch, and it was 8:00 p.m. After counting, I realized that in forty-five minutes I had written only 143 acceptable words. Returning to my prayer closet, I said, "Lord, at this rate You will have come back to earth before this book ever gets finished! Now, I can think of four alternatives. I can put it up for tonight and say that I am too tired to write. Or, You could dictate to me here in my prayer closet the way You want this chapter to be written. Or, You could dictate to me at the typewriter. Or, I can keep on struggling. What do You want me to do?"

I waited. After a while, I looked at my watch, and it was 8:15 p.m. Again, I said, "Please, Lord, don't keep me waiting. I have so little time as it is. Please help me." Just then I heard Him say, "Go to your typewriter." I obeyed.

Immediately upon putting the paper in my typewriter, I began to hear His voice. I typed furiously. Eight pages were dictated to me as fast as I could write. The muscle in my right arm began to ache a bit, and the Holy Spirit said, "You are getting too tired to type more tonight. Put it up, and we'll finish later." Looking at my watch, I saw that it was exactly 9:00 p.m.—forty-five minutes of dictation from God!

When I got all of the pages straightened and counted the words, there were nearly 5,000! I took the pages upstairs to show my husband, who is my "par excellence" editor. When I told him my experience, he said, "Let me read it." I gave him the pages and returned to my office.

As I entered the room, the Lord spoke clearly and said, "Mary Ruth, I have tried for years to get you to let Me help you with your work, but you wouldn't listen. You have been such a hard worker, plodding along at full speed, hardly ever asking Me for help. If you would just let Me help, you could accomplish so much more." Knowing it was the truth, I put my head on my office desk and with tears apologized to the Lord.

Thirty minutes later, Don came to my office, handed me the pages and said, "It's beautiful. I couldn't change a noun, a verb, an adjective, or an adverb. I am sure your readers will be deeply touched by this part of the book." I knew he was right.

You Can Count On The Lord

You might be thinking, Does God always work like that? I would have to answer, "No, He doesn't. At least He doesn't for me." If He did, this book could have been written in a matter of hours instead of the many months it has taken me to research and organize my ideas. But I don't mind searching through the library to find the biographies of famous saints or flipping through concordances, reference Bibles, and other "helps" necessary to complete the work the Lord has asked me to do.

When I put forth my best effort, God does what I cannot do—and receiving His help is always thrilling. When I see what great things God has done, "high praise" flows from my heart, usually accompanied by tears of joy.

Over the years, the Lord has often spoken to me concerning my work and the talents He has given me. As a word of encouragement to you, let me share some of these special messages:

> "I will work closely with you at all times because I want you to succeed. This is My work. I will maximize your talents, for this is My divine plan. I am able to magnify the abilities and the talents of any human being who dedicates himself completely to My will. Rejoice constantly that you can be numbered among those who have been chosen for special service in the Kingdom.
>
> "No credit for this belongs to you, of course, for all you did was to obey the spiritual rules laid down in the foundation of life and of living. Rejoice anyway, for you will enjoy great and wonderful pleasures as you die to self and live unto Me. My ways shall be magnified even more as you stay yielded to My plan and as you seek My will in your daily walk."

Will He do the same for you? Yes! Whatever your field of endeavor, I believe God wants to help you attain mastery in it—for His glory. Ask Him to show you how best to work. He wants to give you the spirit of wisdom and multiply your God-given talents.

Making Right Decisions

Most of us have trouble with one area of life that we cannot escape—making decisions. Every day we have to decide what to do, when to do it, and how to do it. One wrong decision can wreck a lifelong career or throw a family into financial disaster.

While making decisions is never easy, there is one way we can always know we have made the correct choice—by listening for God's guidance concerning the matter. He wants to be our Guide through this life. "For this God is our God for ever and ever: he will be our guide even unto death" (Psalm 48:14).

The book of James makes it clear that God will help us make wise decisions as long we seek His wisdom with an attitude of expectancy.

> If you want to know what God wants you to do, ask him, and he will gladly tell you, for he is always ready to give a bountiful supply of wisdom to all who ask him; he will not resent it. But when you ask him, be sure that you really expect him to tell you, for a doubtful mind will be as unsettled as a wave of the sea that is driven and tossed by the wind; and every decision you then make will be uncertain, as you turn first this way, and then that. If you don't ask with faith, don't expect the Lord to give you any solid answer—James 1:5-8, *TLB*.

Since I established a prayer closet as my place to pray and have included listening prayer as a regular part of my prayer time, I almost never make a decision without first consulting with my heavenly Guide. God's guidance through personal words, visions, dreams, and Scripture have helped me make important decisions and fulfill His plan for my life.

When The Answer Is No

While I was still working as a university dean, I received a phone call from Washington, D.C., asking if I would accept the nomination for an important office in a national professional association. Although I was pleased and excited, at the same time I was exceedingly busy in my own work and desperately working toward an early retirement. I truly wanted and needed the Lord's direction—not my own good judgment.

This day was already heavily scheduled with appointments, and I didn't have time to shut myself off for a time of prayer. I said, "Lord, I need an answer right away. I know You will understand, and You know I want only Your will in this matter."

When I opened my Bible, my eyes fell on Proverbs 5:11, "Lest afterwards you groan in anguish and in shame" (*TLB*). I felt that the answer was "no," but I wasn't positive. So I asked the Lord for further confirmation, and my eyes fell on the words, "Drink from your own well" (verse 15). This seemed to mean that I should not over-extend myself by getting involved in outside endeavors.

Then I read, "For God is closely watching you and he weighs carefully everything you do." On the opposite page I read, "Listen, son of mine, to what I say. Listen carefully. Keep these thoughts ever in mind" (Proverbs 4:20, *TLB*).

I was almost convinced that God was saying I should not accept the nomination. Then my assistant dean came to work, and I told her about my offer. She strongly encouraged me to change my mind. She gave me several excellent reasons why I would be good for this position and how it would benefit both me and the university.

Almost immediately, a former faculty member who understood the whole situation phoned long distance. Her response to my situation settled the matter for sure. She said, "Dean Swope, you told me in Boston last June that you wanted to do more work for the Lord. If you take this office, you know your time will be completely committed to professional pursuits. I feel strongly that you should not accept."

My answer to the committee was, "Thanks, but no thanks!" Since that time, I have never wondered if I made the right decision.

Listen To Me

Just before my retirement in 1980, I was especially pressured in my work. In addition to keeping up with a daily job, I needed to clean out twenty-four drawers of accumulated professional archives.

One morning I awakened at five o'clock and after a time of prayer went to work at 6:30. Just looking at the pile of material on my desk from the day before gave me a sinking feeling in the pit of my stomach.

I got my Bible, held it up to the Lord and said, "Please, Father. Show me where to read to get a lift in my spirit." The word "Isaiah" was sparked in my mind like lightning. I said, "Fine. What chapter?" I immediately heard, "Fifty-One." After turning there, my eyes fell on these words:

> Listen to me, all who hope for deliverance, who seek the Lord! . . . You worry about being so small . . . Abraham was only one when I called him. But when I blessed him, he became a great nation. . . . Listen to me, my people . . . My mercy and justice are coming soon; your salvation is on the way. . . . Rise up and robe yourself with strength. . . . I, even I, am he who comforts you and gives you all this joy—Isaiah 51:1-12, *TLB*.

Needless to say, I was energized by that Word from the Lord. A few days later, I was facing a meeting with the New Programs Committee of the Board of Higher Education. This was the eighth time I was having to defend the reasons for a new Master's Degree program. Approval of this program was very important to me since it would be my last contribution to curriculum development before leaving my university post.

The day before, one of the vice presidents had seen me on campus and said, "I guess you know, Dean

Swope, that you're not going to get approval for your new M. A. in Gerontology program tomorrow." I asked him why he said that, and he answered, "Because it has become a political football on campus, and too many other departments are out for their piece of the action."

I disagreed but told him we would know in another twenty-four hours. His remarks depressed me a bit. As the only female academic Dean, I often found competing in an all-male environment difficult.

When I returned to my office, I asked the Lord to give me a verse that would counsel me on the matter. Again I heard, "Turn to Isaiah 51." When I did, my eyes fell on verse four: "Listen to me, my people; listen . . . for I will see that right prevails." I closed the Bible for, that was all I wanted in the first place—for right to prevail.

Are you surprised to learn that the next day the Board of Higher Education voted in my favor?

Appropriating God's Wisdom

All true wisdom comes from God, who is the source of all wisdom. "For the Lord giveth wisdom: out of his mouth cometh knowledge and understanding" (Proverbs 2:6). Every born-again believer in the Lord Jesus Christ can appropriate God's wisdom in their life. "But of him are ye in Christ Jesus, who of God is made unto us wisdom" (1 Corinthians 1:30).

God has given us His Spirit to make us wise in every area of our lives—in our work, our relationships, and our ministry. Paul told the Colossian believers:

> Ever since we first heard about you we have kept on praying and asking God to help you understand what he wants you to do; asking him to make you wise about spiritual things; and asking that the way you live will always please the Lord and honor him, so that you will always be doing good, kind things for others, while all the time you are learning to know God better and better—Colossians 1:9-10, *TLB*.

As you ask God to give you the spirit of wisdom, your work will be done with greater skill, your decisions will be wiser, and your life will be more pleasing to God. No wonder Jesus said He came to give us life more abundantly!

Let me close this chapter with some messages I received from the Lord concerning the spirit of wisdom and His desire to help us in every area of life.

> "There is no need for any child of Mine to be without the knowledge and the truth he needs to do My work. It is My plan that all of you have the tools you need. *You* are no exception to this statement.

"Believers know that I am all wisdom and all knowledge. I have the answers to every human problem, be it physical, emotional, or mental. I can tell you everything about everything that is to be known. What are your greatest and most perplexing questions? Ask Me, for I long to tell you the answers you will need in order to magnify My name. Let it be revealed to you through the Holy Spirit.

"Come, therefore, to the Fountainhead of all knowledge, and ask whatever you want to know, whatever you need to know. Knowledge is as easy to flow down the river of life as any other commodity necessary to meet your human needs. Ask. Go ahead, ask. I am waiting to answer your questions."

CHAPTER NINE

The Right To Be Guided

If you are a born-again believer in Jesus Christ, you have already heard God's voice. Jesus said, "No man can come to me, except the Father which hath sent me draw him" (John 6:44). The Holy Spirit got your attention, brought conviction, and urged you to repent. You "were called," or you never would have yielded.

The Holy Spirit got the attention of William Murray, son of atheist Madalyn Murray O'Hair, and led him to the truth he had been seeking. In his book, *My Life Without God,* William Murray recalls the miraculous intervention of God in his life.

> On the night of January 24, 1980, an unusual event changed my life. I went to bed and, not long after falling asleep, experienced a consuming nightmare of unmentionable horror. Suddenly, the nightmare was sliced in half by a mighty,

gleaming sword of gold and silver. The two halves of the nightmare peeled back as if a black and white photograph had been cut in half. A great winged angel stood with the sword in his hand. The blade of the sword pointed down, making it resemble a cross. On one of the sword's hilts was inscribed the words *"in hoc signo vince."* The tip of the sword's blade touched an open Bible.

Then I awoke, realizing that my quest for the truth would end within the page of the Holy Bible, the very book my family had helped ban from devotional use in the public schools of America.

Wide awake, I climbed out of bed, dressed, and drove into San Francisco. Despite what any psychiatrist's interpretation might be, I believed this dream had told me two things. First, the answers to most if not all of my personal problems and dilemmas were in the book the sword had touched—the Bible. Second, only through the cross would I be able to conquer these problems (*in hoc signo vince* translates, "by this symbol conquer.")

I drove to an all-night discount department store near Fisherman's Wharf. There, under a stack of porno magazines in the "literature" section, I found a Bible.

I drove to my apartment and read the book of the Bible written by the great physician, Luke. There I found my answer—not the book itself, but Jesus Christ. I had heard many times in various churches that all one needed to do was to admit guilt and ask Jesus in. I had not made that one step, to ask Him into my heart. I knew I must take that step, and I did so that night. God was no longer a distant, impersonal "force." I now knew Him in a personal way.

Within days my life and attitudes began to change. I read in the Bible that anything asked in Jesus' name in prayer would be answered. On January 25, I asked God to remove from me the desire to drink alcohol. The desire left. Later I asked that the chains of my three-packs-a-day cigarette habit be broken. As if by a miracle, the desire for tobacco passed and along with it the bronchitis I had suffered with from my youth.

More importantly, though, my hatred began to vanish as the love of Christ took over my being. I no longer intensely hated my mother. Now I really wanted to be able to love her, whereas before I had only wanted revenge. I began to see my mother for what she truly was—a sinner, just like me.

Although your conversion experience may not have been as dramatic, I'm sure you can remember the little nudgings and the gentle pulling of the

Holy Spirit on your heart. God was speaking to you even then—before you ever accepted Jesus as your Savior.

Twelve Points To Remember

Since your re-birth experience, you have probably received definite and specific guidance from God many times. The scriptures teach that this is the covenant-right of every child of God. "I will instruct thee and teach thee in the way which thou shalt go. I will guide thee with mine eye" (Psalm 32:8).

We can confidently expect to receive guidance from God every time we seek His direction. He wants to help us make correct decisions and fulfill His plan for our lives.

Loren Cunningham, founder and director of *Youth With A Mission,* has been receiving God's direction for many years. He has taught hundreds, if not thousands, of people how to hear from God. In his book, *Is That Really You God?*, Loren gives "twelve points to remember" when hearing the voice of God.

1. Don't make guidance complicated. It is actually hard *not* to hear God if you really want to please and obey Him! . . .

Here are three simple steps that have helped us to hear God's voice:

SUBMIT to His Lordship. Ask Him to help you silence your own thoughts, desires, and the opinions of others. . . . You want to hear only the thoughts of the Lord . . . (Proverbs 3:5-6).

RESIST the enemy. . . . Use the authority which Jesus Christ has given you to silence the voice of the enemy. (James 4:7; Ephesians 6:10-20).

EXPECT an answer. After asking a question that is on your mind, wait for Him to answer. Expect your loving heavenly Father to speak to you. He will (John 10:27; Psalm 69:13; Exodus 33:11).

2. Allow God to speak to you in the *way* He chooses. Don't try to dictate to Him concerning the guidance methods you prefer. . . . Listen with a yielded heart; there is a direct link between yieldedness and hearing. He may choose to speak to you: through *His Word* . . . through an *audible voice* . . . through *dreams* and *visions*. . . . But probably the most common of all means is through the quiet *inner voice* (Isaiah 30:21).

3. Confess any unforgiven sin. A clean heart is a prerequisite to hearing God. (Psalm 66:18).

4. . . . Have you obeyed the last thing God told you to do?

5. Get your own leading. God will use others to confirm your guidance but you should also hear from Him directly. . . . (1 Kings 13).

6. Don't talk about your guidance until God gives you permission to do so. . . . The main purpose of waiting is to help you avoid four pitfalls of guidance: pride . . . presumption . . . missing God's timing and method . . . bringing confusion to others.

7. . . . God will often use two or more spiritually sensitive people to confirm what He is telling you (2 Corinthians 13:1).

8. Beware of counterfeits. . . . Satan has a counterfeit for everything of God that is possible for him to copy (Acts 8:9-11). . . .

9. Opposition of man is sometimes guidance from God (Acts 21:10-12). . . . The important thing here, again, is yieldedness to the Lord. . . . Rebellion is never of God. . . .

10. Every follower of Jesus has a unique ministry (1 Corinthians 12; 1 Peter 4:10-11). The more you seek to hear God's voice in detail, the more effective you will be in your own calling. . . .

11. Practice hearing God's voice and it becomes easier. It's like picking up the phone and recognizing the voice of your friend . . . you know his voice because you have heard it so much. . . .

12. Relationship is the most important reason for hearing the voice of God. . . . If you don't have communication, you don't have a personal relationship with Him.

True guidance . . . is getting closer to the Guide. We grow to know the Lord better as He speaks to us and, as we listen to Him and obey, we make His heart glad. (Exodus 33:11; Matthew 7:24-27).

Waiting For The Answer

Although I just recently read Loren Cunningham's book, I have, over the years, put these principles into practice in my listening-prayer experience. *Waiting* is often the hardest part of receiving God's guidance. But, as Loren Cunningham said, waiting helps prevent many pitfalls. The last thing you want to do is run ahead of God and miss not only His perfect timing but the perfect method He wants to use.

Let me share how the Lord guided me through one of the biggest steps of faith my husband and I had ever taken.

Immediately upon retirement in 1980, Don and I planned a vacation trip to Florida. On the way we attended a Founder's Seminar sponsored by Pat Robertson and the Christian Broadcasting Network in Virginia Beach, Virginia.

After Pat had preached to the participants one morning, he asked us to think of something we would like to achieve for God that was well beyond our ability. I thought for a moment and then made my request. I asked God to help me give, through our new ministry, the same amount of money I had earned in salary my last year at the university.

The group was quiet for a few minutes. Suddenly Pat began to speak, using one of the gifts of the Spirit—the word of knowledge. He revealed two or three requests that people had made, saying that God would answer them.

Then Pat said, "Someone here has asked God for a rather large sum of money." After a short pause, he spoke again of my request and named the exact amount that I had earned last year!

At that moment, faith exploded in my heart, and I knew God was going to enable us to give that specific amount to His work. I envisioned myself being overwhelmed with seminar requests and flooded with book royalty checks. But God's ways are not are our ways.

Almost nothing was achieved financially that first year. In fact, I had to wait *four years* before I saw my request answered.

An Unexpected Miracle

In January 1984, Don and I were to return to CBN for another seminar. Before going, I went to my prayer closet to ask the Lord how much Don and I should pledge toward the World Outreach Center. I knew we would be given an opportunity to help support this work while we were at CBN. Although I received no definite word from the Lord, I had a specific amount in mind.

At the same time I was praying, Don was in another part of the house seeking the Lord's will in this matter. When I went to him and told him the amount

I had in mind, he said, "I was thinking twice that amount." This really surprised me, for we almost always agreed on financial matters. Since he is the head of our house, I agreed with him. But I had no idea where the money would come from!

We went to CBN in Virginia Beach. After an evening session, Don said to me, "I feel impressed to sign our pledge card for a higher amount—in fact, two and one-half times higher!"

Immediately I answered, "Well, I didn't have faith for your first pledge, so I certainly can't have faith for this amount. Nonetheless, it is fine with me. Go ahead and make the larger pledge." So we did.

To show how God supplied the money we had pledged, I need to go back to August 1983. I was a guest on the "Getting Together" TV program, aired by the Christian station in Pittsburgh and hosted by Russ and Norma Bixler. That evening we discussed the problem of arteriosclerosis (plugged-up arteries) and a new oral chelation pill that can help alleviate this condition.

After the show, Russ told me that God had spoken to him while I was talking and said, "You have this condition, and you need to start this treatment." As a supplier of the product, I was able to provide it for Russ, and he began oral chelation therapy that very day.

When Russ wrote and asked if I could be on the show again in February 1984, I agreed. (This was one month after we had made our pledge to CBN.) I wrote that I would like to discuss the chapter in my book dealing with self-denial of unneeded calories. When Russ didn't object, I went to Pittsburgh fully prepared to discuss this topic.

The day of the program, Russ had just returned from a trip to Philadelphia. His late arrival at the station gave us no time to talk before the show. The producer was counting—9,8,7,6 . . . , when I asked Russ, "Are we going to talk about self-denial of calories?"

"No," he replied, "I want to talk about chelation therapy."

For twenty-five minutes Russ and Norma testified about how our product had helped him. Russ no longer had cold hands and feet, and he could climb a hill without pains in his legs. His angina pain was totally gone, and the tingling feeling in his hands had been healed. At the end of the show, Russ gave the viewing audience my address and suggested that they write to me for more information about oral chelation therapy.

When I returned home, mail from Pennsylvania started flooding in. The first day we had 164 letters; second day 259; third day 309; fourth day 464! Our lives were completely changed overnight. We quickly had to set up an office, employ people, work out business procedures, answer letters, and fill orders for our vitamin/mineral/amino acid/herb product.

Through the totally unexpected sales of the oral chelation tablets, God exceeded our CBN pledge by 5000 percent! Because of Don's faith, not mine, we were able to give to Great Commission projects and programs about $8,000 above my last earned salary.

In God's own time and totally by His own methods, my prayer request made in 1980 was answered in 1984. Praise the Lord!

Your Covenant-Right

As a born-again child of God, it is your covenant-right to be guided by the Holy Spirit. Listen to this word from the Lord telling how He feels about this matter of guidance:

> "Surely you know by now that I am more than willing to direct your affairs and keep your activities in line with My will and plan for your life. Keep asking your questions and expecting the answers. There is no need to be in darkness over anything—you can walk in all the light you want. Continue to ask for guidance and for the leading of the Holy Spirit in your life."

As you ask to be guided and led by the Lord, one thing is for sure—you can expect miracles to happen in your life!

Expect Miracles

MIRACLES are on the way!
Miracles of salvation,
Miracles of achievement,
Miracles of healing,
Miracles of believing,

Miracles of the mind.
Spiritual miracles are on the way,
Physical miracles are on the way,
Miracles of speech are on the way,
Miracles of thought are on the way,
Miracles of love are being poured out,
Miracles of deliverance are being sent,
Miracles of creativity are flowing down
    like confetti at a time of celebration!
Look up! Reach out! Embrace them all!
Rejoice. Praise Me.
Exclaim praises from deep within.
Hear My voice.
See My miracle working power as
    supernatural and altogether lovely.
Praise Me.
Yes, praise Me!

CHAPTER TEN
Sovereignly Revealed Secrets

The Bible clearly teaches that God reveals secrets, but He also withholds knowledge from us for various reasons. Moses told the children of Israel, "There are secrets the Lord your God has not revealed to us, but these words which he has revealed are for us and our children to obey forever" (Deuteronomy 29:29, *TLB*).

It is our responsibility to obey the words the Lord has spoken to us, and it is our privilege to trust Him for the secrets He has not revealed. Let's look at how God reveals His secrets to us and why He sometimes withholds certain knowledge.

The Secret Method

How does God reveal secrets? The apostle Paul tells us the method God uses to reveal His deepest thoughts to His children:

Eye hath not see, nor ear heard, neither have entered into the heart of man, the things which God hath prepared for them that love him. But God hath revealed them unto us by his Spirit: for the Spirit searcheth all things, yea, the deep things of God— 1 Corinthians 2:9-10.

The Living Bible says the Holy Spirit shows us "God's deepest secrets." How does God reveal His secrets to man? By the Holy Spirit. To the listening-prayer seeker, the most reassuring words in Scripture are found in John 16:13-14:

"When the Holy Spirit, who is truth, comes, he shall guide you into all truth, for he will not be presenting his own ideas, but will be passing on to you what he has heard. He will tell you about the future. He shall praise me and bring me great honor by showing you my glory"—John 16:13-14, *TLB*.

We know we can trust the secrets the Holy Spirit reveals to us because He is speaking only the words of God—and God only reveals what *He* wants to reveal. "Having made known unto us the mystery of his will, *according to his good pleasure* which he hath purposed in himself: that in the dispensation of the fulness of times he might gather together in one all things in Christ" (Ephesians 1:9-10, *italics added*).

In most instances, God's plan is one of gradual revelation. When the time was right, God sent Jesus into the world and revealed Him as the Savior of mankind. "The mystery of the gospel" was kept a secret until God's timing was perfectly fulfilled. Even God's plan for offering salvation to the Gentiles was kept a mystery from the beginning of time. No one would have believed it anyway! In fact, God had to practically hit Peter over the head to get him to see that the Gentiles could be saved and filled with the Holy Spirit.

Our finite, simple minds cannot comprehend the greatness of God or even fathom the wonders of what it means to be His children. The apostle John wrote, "We are already God's children, right now, and we can't even imagine what it is going to be like later on. But we do know this, that when he comes we will be like him, as a result of seeing him as he really is" (1 John 3:2, *TLB*).

Many spiritual truths will become clear to us only when we get to heaven. It is not that God refuses to reveal them to us but that our minds cannot assimilate such knowledge—it is too wonderful for us to comprehend.

His Sovereign Pleasure

God is the sovereign ruler of the universe. "Our God is in the heavens: he hath done whatsoever he hath pleased" (Psalm 115:3). No amount of begging and pleading or fasting and praying can force God to reveal anything He does not want to reveal. Nothing we can do will make Him tell us something before it is time for us to know it.

When Jesus washed the disciples' feet, He told them they were unable at that time to understand why He was doing this but that later on it would be clear to them. (See John 13:1-7.) God sometimes withholds knowledge or revelation from us because of our present inability to comprehend it.

At other times, our human frailty makes it necessary for God to restrain from showing us things that we are unable to handle emotionally. Jesus told His disciples that He had much more to tell them, but they could not bear it at that time. (See John 16:12.) God graciously does not reveal certain things to us because He knows such knowledge would create fear or make us lose heart.

God knows that we are like little children who, if given the chance, will take the paint brush and smear the canvas before He can even perfect the design. Because we cannot see the entire picture, advance knowledge about a situation might cause us to rush ahead of God and spoil everything. Not being completely informed makes it necessary for us to trust the Lord and believe that He has everything under control. The apostle Paul had the kind of faith that says, "God, I trust You." He wrote:

> We can see and understand only a little about God now, as if we were peering at his reflection in a poor mirror; but someday we are going to see him in his completeness, face to face. Now all that I know is hazy and

blurred, but then I will see everything clearly, just as clearly as God sees into my heart right now—1 Corinthians 13:12, *TLB*.

When God, in His sovereignty, reveals only a portion of His will, can you trust Him for the rest, knowing that He has your best interests in mind? The more you learn to trust Him, the more He will trust you to know.

The Lord sometimes reveals profound mysteries beyond man's understanding. God revealed to Daniel King Nebuchadnezzar's vision and its meaning—what was to happen in the future. This is something Daniel could not have known without divine revelation.

In His sovereignty, God also sometimes reveals secrets that are beyond our scope of knowledge. This has happened to me a few times.

For several years, I had problems with my fingernails chipping and splitting. More than one doctor gave me advice and tried to help, but nothing worked.

One night I was awakened from sleep to hear a male voice saying very clearly, "Take fresh zinc for your fingernail problem." I wondered, Where would you find fresh zinc?

A few days later I came across a product called Barley Green, a powder made from the leaves of the barley plant, which contains generous amounts of zinc. It is "fresh" in that the leaves are gathered immediately, made into juice, and then in two to three seconds are spray-dried into a concentrate.

I started taking two teaspoons of Barley Green daily, and my fingernails were almost totally healed in five weeks!

The Path Revealed

After my retirement, I continued to seek God's will concerning the work He had for me to do. During my prayer times, the Lord often spoke to me and said:

> "I will reveal the path you should take, and I will work closely with you at all times. I want you to succeed because this is My work. I am preparing audiences to hear the word I want you to deliver. I am preparing the hearts of many who will listen and who will hear. I will maximize your talents, for this is My divine plan."

In November 1983, my husband and I attended a seminar at the Christian Retreat Center, Bradenton, Florida. On Saturday morning, I got up early to attend the women's prayer group before leaving for home. During that meeting, a woman said to the leader, "I have a message for the lady sitting across from me." The leader suggested that she come over to where I was sitting and tell me about it.

The woman said, "Just now in a vision I saw you walking down the middle of a very wide, long, emerald-green highway. On either side of the road were doors—large and small, made of all types of wood and metal. They were beautiful, unique doors.

All of a sudden, one hand-carved door with a beautiful brass knob opened from the inside, and you walked through it. God told me to tell you that He is going to open a new door for you soon; He wants you to walk through it unafraid.''

All of the ladies present gathered around me and prayed for a special blessing on my life.

When I went to the motel lobby to meet my husband, he said, ''Remember the lady we met last night at the service? She has something very important to tell you. She is at the swimming pool and wants you to come out there before we leave.''

As I approached the pool area, she saw me coming and jumped up from her lounge chair to meet me. She said, ''When I returned to my room last night after the service, I had a vision about you. I saw you going down a long hallway, and there were all kinds of doors on either side— large and small ones, unique and expensive ones, and others that were plain but beautiful. The Lord told me to tell you that He is going to open doors for you soon and that He wants you to go through each one as you have the opportunity. He said to tell you that He is going to use you to bring glory to His name in many places, both large and small.''

I was excited to have received the same message from two different women who did not know me or each other. My excitement intensified two months later when I attended a seminar on the Holy Spirit. Near the beginning of an evening service, the leader said, "Will the lady with the white hair and the blue suit come here, please. I have a word from the Lord for you."

When I went forward, he spoke in tongues for a minute or two and then said:

"Daughter, while others have gone the way you have gone and are ready to retire, I say to you that you are ready to *refire*. I have redirected you with My anointing. You are going to do Kingdom work, and you will accomplish more for the Lord than many will have done in a lifetime. You are going to be effective for me.

"I am going to open doors in different areas. You are going to start out teaching on the natural. You will teach many things in nutrition, but this will be a vehicle, an open door, to minister the spiritual.

"The doors I am going to open will not just be in churches. I am going to open doors in health centers, in universities, and other areas. I am going to give you an interview on TV. You will be a seed sower— the good seed—the kind that consumes a person. Later you will meet people who will tell you that their lives have been changed by your teaching."

This word came through a stranger—a man I did not know and had never met. In my heart, I knew it was a word from God.

The Emerald-Green Highway

The first fulfillment of this special message came three weeks later when I was interviewed by Russ and Norma Bixler on the "Getting Together" TV program in Pittsburgh. I have already shared with you the financial miracle that God began for us that night.

Doors of service began to open almost immediately. Within six months, I appeared on six different television and radio talk shows in various parts of the country. In addition, I was asked to give numerous speeches and seminars. Doors opened without help from me in any way, as I had been told they would.

The emerald-green highway aspect of the vision remained a mystery, however, until October 1985 when I heard about a product from Japan called Barley Green. Immediately, I was excited about the possibility of its filling one of the missing links in our American diet—the lack of deep-green leafy vegetables.

The National Research Council has maintained for years that we need 1/2 cup daily of a dark-green leafy or yellow vegetable to meet our need for beta-carotene and vitamin A. Notoriously absent from the American diet are such foods as Swiss chard, collards, turnip greens, kale, beet greens, squash, pumpkin, sweet potatoes, and carrots.

Upon further investigation, I found that the researcher who discovered the nutritional value of Barley Green had made a momentous statement. He said, "My research has shown that the embryonic leaves of the barley plant contain the most prolific source of all the nutrients in a balanced form in a single food on the face of the earth."

That statement, along with other supporting documentation in his book, *Green Barley Essence,* made me question whether or not I should get involved in the sale of the product. This need for wisdom sent me seeking divine guidance.

The answer came painlessly in a very interesting setting. While attending the Women's Aglow International Convention in Anaheim in late October, CBN President Pat Robertson addressed the delegates. As a part of his message, he said, "If Jesus were to appear in the convention center tonight, all 8,000 women present would rush forward to ask Him at least two very pressing questions for which you have no answer." Then he added, "Jesus is here right now. My faith tells me that if you ask your questions and listen for Him to speak, the Holy Spirit will give you God's answer. Let's stand and be quiet for fifteen minutes while you ask God for the answer to two of your most pressing questions."

My first question was answered instantaneously with one single word, which I heard in my spirit. I was thrilled. Then I asked, "Lord, do You want me to be involved with Barley Green or not?" After several minutes of silence, I heard, "Go for it." Thinking that I had heard the answer, I opened my eyes and began looking around, but God had not finished speaking to me.

In about two more minutes, the words, "Full speed ahead," were audibly spoken. I got my notebook and wrote both sentences so I could be precise in recalling exactly what I heard.

In another few minutes I heard, "The way is clear." And lastly, the Holy Spirit said so emphatically, "There are no hindrances."

About two weeks after the convention, I read in Leviticus during my normal Bible reading:

> "*The Festival of Firstfruits:* When you arrive in the land I will give you and reap your first harvest, bring the first sheaf of the harvest to the priest on the day after the Sabbath. He shall wave it before the Lord in a gesture of offering, and it will be accepted by the Lord as your gift"— Leviticus 23:9-11, *TLB*.

Upon further study, I discovered that God chose barley leaves as the wave offering for the Festival of Firstfruits. That was exciting. Then I learned from a friend who has attended six of these festivals in Israel that barley is still being used today. I knew in my spirit that barley leaves had special significance!

Two weeks later, when I was in my prayer closet, I asked, "Lord, is there anything You want to say to me today?"

Immediately, I heard, "Mary Ruth, who is the real Firstfruits?"

I quickly replied, "I don't know, Lord." Then, like a flash, the Scripture verse about Jesus being the Firstfruits of those to be raised from the dead came to my mind. So, I said, "Oh, I know, it's Jesus!"

Then the Holy Spirit said, "You are right. What Jesus is to the spirit, barley leaves are to the body."

Suddenly, my mind was filled with many ideas. Jesus is Savior, Healer, Deliverer, and Redeemer. I left that prayer closet yearning to share the benefits of Barley Green with every person I possibly could. This super-nutrition preventive of disease could also be a healer to those already suffering with conditions caused by malnutrition.

Today my entire family is involved in selling this marvelous, natural product. I am presently writing a new book about Barley Green and how it can prevent and heal disease. No wonder I feel as if I am traveling down the middle of a beautiful emerald-green highway with doors opening on both sides, just as God said they would.

I look forward to each new year with more excitement than I had in any of my previous sixty-six years. I feel like shouting from the housetops, "Praise the Lord! His mercies are new every morning, and His kindnesses endure forever."

God in His sovereignty revealed His secret plans for my life according to "His good pleasure" and not mine—because *He is God*.

God Has A Plan For Your Life

Seek God's will for your life. You know He has a plan. Don't stop short of hearing directly from Him about what it is. Be faithful, and your reward will far outweigh the trouble and discomfort of being still to hear Him speak. Listen to this word from the Lord:

"I am ready and willing to reveal much more to you about My plan for the rest of your life than you have been willing to sit still long enough to receive. Spend time in quiet meditation. I want to commune with you and satisfy your soul with good things from the Throne itself. Get quiet before Me and read My Word. Listen for My voice, and you will experience the *knowing* that comes to the spirit and on through the soul to your complete understanding."

Lay hold, therefore, of God's willingness to communicate His secrets to you. Prove to yourself and your world that all who are "of the truth" hear His voice.

CHAPTER ELEVEN
Dreams And Visions

The biographies of great preachers and saints are filled with supernatural experiences. Recorded throughout the pages of their lives are incidents in which God revealed His thoughts and intentions to them. These men and women were led and guided by God speaking to them in one of the many ways He communicates with His children.

During the last two centuries, God produced some remarkable "spiritual giants," including John and Charles Wesley, Jonathan Edwards, John "Praying" Hyde, Hudson Taylor, Charles Finney, and many others. If you study their lives, you will find that these godly believers, who did great exploits for the Kingdom, had a life-long practice of *waiting upon God.* They were willing to spend whole nights and long hours in the day seeking God. For them, fulfillment in life came primarily through the disciplines of godliness, which required much time spent alone before the Lord.

In his memoirs, Charles G. Finney, the great revival preacher of the nineteenth century, writes about a vision he had after a long night of prayer.

> The day was just beginning to dawn. But all at once a light perfectly ineffable shone in my soul, that almost prostrated me to the ground. In this light it seemed as if I could see that all nature praised and worshipped God except man. This light seemed to be like the brightness of the sun in every direction. It was too intense for the eyes. I recollect casting my eyes down and breaking into a flood of tears, in view of the fact that mankind did not praise God. I think I knew something then, by actual experience, of that light that prostrated Paul on his way to Damascus. It was surely a light such as I could not have endured long. . . .
>
> I saw the glory of God; and . . . I could not endure to think of the manner in which He was treated by men. Indeed, it did not seem to me at the time that the vision of His glory which I had, was to be described in words. I wept it out; and the vision, if it may be so called, passed away and left my mind calm.

Modern-day Christians, when compared with the saints of earlier times, appear to have lost the art of possessing quietness of soul—one of the main requirements of listening prayer. Our minds and ears

are so preoccupied with instruments of sound—
television, radio, tape players, stereos, etc.—that we
have never developed the discipline of quiet
listening.

How can we, in our generation, find a quiet place
and adequate time to have conversation with God?
The only way I know to find time for waiting upon
God is through the lonely valley of self-denial and
personal discipline. If there is another way, it has not
been revealed from heaven and, to my knowledge,
it has not been successfully demonstrated upon
earth.

Revealing The Future

In Bible times, God often spoke to His prophets
and servants through dreams and visions. Joseph and
Daniel are well-known examples of how God used
dreams and visions to reveal the future and bring
wisdom in times of need.

In these last days before Christ's return, God
says, "I will pour out my spirit upon all flesh;
and your sons and daughters shall prophesy, your
old men shall dream dreams, your young men shall
see visions" (Joel 2:28). As more and more believers
learn to listen to God in prayer, we can expect
to have more dreams and see more visions than ever
before.

Derek Prince, a well-known missionary and con-
ference speaker, tells about a vision given during a
large gathering of believers in Kenya, East Africa, in
1960:

After the close of the missionary's address the Holy Spirit moved with sovereign power and lifted the meeting onto a supernatural plane. For the next two hours almost the whole group of more than two hundred people continued in spontaneous worship and prayer, without any visible human leadership.

At a certain point the conviction came to me that, as a group, we had touched God, and that His power was at our disposal. God spoke to my spirit, and said, " . . . Tell them to pray for the future of Kenya."

I began to make my way to the platform, intending to deliver to the whole group the message which I felt God had given me. On the way I passed Lydia, who was sitting beside the aisle. She put out her hand and stopped me.

"What do you want?" I asked her.

"Tell them to pray for Kenya," she said.

"That's just what I'm going up to the platform for," I replied. I realized that God spoke to my wife at the same time that He had spoken to me, and I accepted this as confirmation of His direction.

Reaching the platform, I called the whole group to silence, and presented God's challenge to them, " . . . The Bible places upon you, as Christians, the responsibility to pray. . . . Your country is now facing the most critical period in its history. Let us unite together in praying for the future of Kenya."

. . . As I led in prayer, almost every person present joined me in praying out loud. The combined volume of voices rising in prayer reminded me of the passage in Revelation 19:6: "And I heard as it were the voice of a great multitude, and as the voice of many waters, and as the voice of mighty thunderings. . . . " The sound of prayer swelled to a crescendo, then suddenly ceased. It was as if some invisible conductor had brought down his baton.

After a few moments of silence . . . [a leader] stood up and spoke to the congregation. "I want to tell you what the Lord showed me [in a vision] while we were praying. . . . I saw a red horse coming toward Kenya from the east," he said. "It was very fierce, and there was a very black man riding on it. Behind it were several other horses, also red and fierce. While we were praying, I saw all the horses turn around, and move away toward the north. . . . I asked God to tell me the meaning of what I had seen, and this is what He told me: 'Only the supernatural power of the prayers of my people can turn away the troubles that are coming upon Kenya!' "

For many days after that [Derek Price said] I continued to meditate on what . . . [He] had told us. . . . I gradually came to the conclusion that by this vision God had granted us an assurance that He had heard our prayers for Kenya, and that He would intervene in some definite way on behalf of the country. Subsequent events in Kenya's history have confirmed that this was so.

One of the ministries of the Holy Spirit is that "He will tell you about the future," Jesus said (John 16:13). He will not "predict" the future, but the Holy Spirit will guide us "into all truth" concerning things to come. Knowing what is going to happen in the future gives us confidence and the assurance to boldly carry out the work God has told us to do—whatever our specific calling may be.

The Heavenly Pitcher

There have been times in my life when I needed to know God was going to intervene in a certain situation. Once, through a vision about the future, He calmed my fears and gave me the courage to continue on the path He has prepared for me.

Soon after my first book came off the press, I felt terribly oppressed. The feeling lasted for more than two weeks. Thoughts of defeat kept coming into my mind, such as: "Your book will never sell; even the title, *Nutrition for Christians,* will see to that!

Your family and friends don't like it; only three people out of one hundred and eight sent you a thank you note for their complimentary copy or made any comment at all about it. You spent every weekend, every vacation, and every night possible writing this book, but it was all a waste of time. You should have accepted all those invitations that you turned down during those three years of writing."

One Sunday morning I was so discouraged that I sought out a spiritually-minded young man at church and shared my feeling with him. He said, "Mary Ruth, you have been attacked by a lying spirit of discouragement." While I had never had such a thought, I immediately felt that this young man had told me the truth.

Then he said, "Let me ask you something. Whose book is it? Is it yours or the Lord's?" I had just been confessing in prayer that my book was not mine but God's—that all of the great ideas in it had been gifts to me from Him.

So I could honestly say to my friend, "Jim, this book belongs to God."

Then he said, "If Jesus were here on earth selling your book, do you think it would be a failure?"

I replied, "Of course not."

"Then you have your answer, don't you? Your book sales will not fail; they *cannot* fail. It is an impossibility."

After thanking my friend for his words of encouragement, I entered the sanctuary for the church service. During the singing of praise choruses, I had a vision.

I saw Jesus standing on top of a huge globe of the world. He had a box cradled under His left arm. As I looked more closely, I could see that it was a box of *Nutrition for Christians* books. Suddenly, the lid of the box opened like a jack-in-the-box.

With His right hand, Jesus began pitching books in all directions. The first one went west, out past the California coastline. I knew it would land on an island somewhere, like the Philippines, where I have good friends. Then the Lord said so plainly, "It will go around the world."

The next book was pitched north—and I had the thought that it would land in Europe. Already I had sent one to a friend in England. I could see that there was a chance of a few being sold there.

The third book was tossed to the south and landed in South Carolina. Then, like a baseball player sliding into a base, it slid into Georgia, Mississippi, Alabama, and on into Florida and other states. The fourth book was thrown to the east, and I could see that it landed in New York City. So I received courage from the thought of its being accepted there.

Just then a group of angels saw what Jesus was doing, and they came and grabbed other boxes. After hurriedly ripping them open, they began furiously tossing books in all directions. Immediately, my depression lifted, and I experienced an exhilaration that encouraged me for months.

Today thousands of these books are in homes and stores around the world—in Australia, Europe, Singapore, South America, and in many places, I am sure, that I don't even know about. The rewards for writing and distributing this book have far exceeded my sacrifices and struggles. It has been one of the greatest blessings of my life.

This first book was later revised and renamed, *Are You Sick & Tired of Feeling Sick & Tired*. Today, after three years, it continues to be on my publisher's bestseller list and has sold more than 100,000 copies worldwide.

Called To Intercede

Sometimes the Lord reveals things through dreams that He cannot communicate to us in words. This is especially true when we are not aware of a problem involving another person.

Several months ago, I had a dream in the middle of the night in which I saw one of my very good friends crying uncontrollably. Feeling led to pray for her, I interceded on her behalf.

A few days later at our home church group meeting, I saw my friend and told her about my experience. She asked me what night this had happened. When I told her, she and her husband exclaimed, "That was the night that our son flew into a rage and knocked five big holes in the walls of his bedroom. We needed your prayers, for sure."

A similar incident occurred concerning my daughter. One night I was awakened from a deep sleep after dreaming that Susan was in distress. I prayed for more than three hours because I had no peace when I would quit and try to go back to sleep.

Two days later, Susan phoned and told us about her experience. In the middle of the night, she had been driving alone when she had a strange but severe asthma attack. To make matters worse, it had been snowing, and the roads were extremely slick. She felt she couldn't make it to the hospital without help.

All of a sudden, the attack left with the same strangeness with which it had come, and she arrived safely at her destination. I was so glad I had continued to intercede for Susan. Her guardian angels were on duty, and they never lose a case when we dispatch them through our prayers!

The Counterfeit

Like any other form of guidance, dreams and visions require testing and confirmation from the Lord because they are especially vulnerable to being counterfeited by the enemy. We must always be on the alert and not accept any dream or vision at face value.

Not long ago, I had an unusual dream experience. For three nights in a row I dreamed about snakes. Since I had always connected snakes with sin and Satan, I asked friends and pastors to help me understand what was wrong in my life. I felt certain that God was trying to tell me something. Yet in my heart I knew I was not involved in any kind of deceit or sinful behavior.

Two days after one of these disturbing dreams, I was listening for God to speak to me, and He said:

"Your dreams about the snakes are nothing to be remembered or cherished. Satan would have you confused and confounded. He would muddle your mind and fill your time with worthless thoughts and activities. Even causing you to question your spiritual condition and your relationship with God would be his delight. Have none of it. Fill your mind with pure and holy thoughts instead. Concentrate on inspired writings and creative thoughts. Cast Satan down. Silence his attempts to harass. Take up the pursuit of your duties for the day, and let peace reign in all areas of your life."

From this experience I learned that not all dreams are of God and not all dreams help solve problems or bring us joy. Remember, one of the tests for discerning the voice of God is a deep, inner peace in our hearts. If you feel disturbed or confused after a dream or vision, go to the Lord and ask Him to reveal the true source.

Life-Changing Encounters

Have you ever wondered why some Christians are so committed to their work or ministry? Like the apostle Paul, they probably have had a life-changing encounter with God at some point. If you read the life stories of great men and women of God—both past and present—you will find a time when God revealed to them His plan for their life and ministry.

Loren Cunningham, founder and director of Youth With A Mission, in his book, *Is That Really You, God?*, describes an experience he had as a young man.

> That night after our singing engagement, I returned to the missionary's guest room with its white walls, unadorned except for an island scene in a cheap wooden frame. I lay down on the bed, doubled the pillow under my head and opened my Bible, routinely asking God to speak into my mind.
>
> What happened next was far from routine.
>
> Suddenly, I was looking at a map of the world. Only the map was alive, moving! I sat up. I shook my head, rubbed my eyes. It was a mental movie. I could see all the continents. Waves were crashing onto their shores. Each went onto a continent, then receded, then came up further until it covered the continent completely.
>
> I caught my breath. Then, as I watched, the scene changed. The waves became young people—kids my age and even younger—covering the continents. They were talking to people on street corners and outside bars. They were going from house to house. They were preaching. Everywhere they were caring for people. . . .
>
> Then the scene was gone.

Wow! I thought. *What was that?*

I looked where I had seen waves of young people but saw only the white wall of the guest room with the island print in its wooden frame. Had I imagined the vision or had God shown me the future?

Was that really you, Lord? I wondered, still staring at the wall, amazed. Young people—kids, really—going out as missionaries! What an idea! I thought about the three boys on the out islands and the harm they had done by just being normal kids. If this strange picture really had come from God, there must be a way to avoid problems yet harness youthful energies.

Why, I thought, *did God give me this vision? Was my future somehow linked to the waves of young people?* For a long time I lay there, staring at nothing at all.

One thing was certain. I should tell no one about the vision. Not until I understood what it meant.

After a while, Loren Cunningham *knew* this vision was, in fact, from God. It changed his life and set him on a course that has established one of the most fruitful missionary-outreach programs of this century—Youth With A Mission. Today thousands of young people around the world are sharing their faith and bringing lost souls to Christ through the instruction they have received at YWAM's Discipleship Training Schools.

What About You?

What about you? Have you had a life-changing encounter with almighty God? Has He revealed His plan and purpose for your life?

You may be thinking that God only speaks through dreams and visions to the great "spiritual giants." But you are wrong. God wants to show you His plan for your life. Are you willing to be quiet before God long enough to let Him tell you—or *show* you—what it is?

CHAPTER TWELVE

Straight From The Heart Of God

God has been good to give me hundreds of spiritual experiences in which I have sensed His presence, felt His power, received His personal guidance, and obtained His blessing. Since I established a prayer closet and included listening prayer as a regular part of my prayer time, God has spoken to me about many things. During these times of quiet listening, the Lord has often given me messages—not just personal words for me alone but truths for the body of believers.

This chapter contains several messages straight from the heart of God. As you read, let His words encourage and challenge you in your personal relationship with the Father. He wants to spur you on to greater work in His Kingdom and increase your faith for the future. Your life will never be the same once you decide to seek the Lord faithfully and diligently. Open your ears and your heart.

Take The First Step

"Believe Me, child, you need to grow up in My ways. Too long you have been going to others for your ideas of how to believe and how to behave. Too long you have put limits on Me and on yourself. You look at the mountains and contemplate their height and their complexity, but you fail to begin to climb up their sides and take command.

"Wake up to how Satan is winning in your behavior. You bind your own strength by letting Satan tell you the time isn't right or the conditions aren't what you think they should be. People will be eternally lost because you insist on doing it your way.

"Go, in Jesus name, using Jesus's name, and I will do the work. You take the first step, and I will go before you with a stream of light. And I will come behind you with a push of power. I will stand beside you to protect and encourage. No weapon formed against you shall prosper.

"My leaders are favored with extra guidance and extra unction from above. They need not know frustration and anxiety over their tasks. I am prepared at all times to show them the way. Their big failing is that they assume responsibilities that were meant to be only Mine. It is My plan they are acting out through their lives, not a man-made plan. My plan is to seek and save the lost. Woe to the Pharisees and the hypocrites. Their plan is to be religious, righteous, and pious."

Idol Worship

"Coming from My Throne Room is the message that idol worship is prevalent among American Christians. Little is known about My idea of idol worship. Almost everyone listening to this would find it a shocking statement. But I repeat Myself. Idol worship is very prevalent among your dear ones. What is meant by that statement? Who is being referred to? What measures should be pursued to straighten out the situation?

"There are many things that you are putting far ahead of your desire to seek My will and plan for your earthly existence. All idols, both large and small, stand as monuments that cast a shadow in the realm that they occupy. They block the free flow of every good and perfect gift flowing down from Me. I will not remove the idol in order to bless you anyway. I permit you to be who you want to be even when I disagree with your judgment and decisions.

"This being the case, ask Me to reveal to you and every individual hearing this message what idols are casting shadows on your spiritual enlightenment and understanding. I am not slack about answering with cutting sincerity and honesty.

"Once the idols are removed, quickly go the next step. Ask Me to reveal clearly to you what events or activities should substitute for the sacrificed idols. After all, entertainment is not all bad. Maybe something you would decide to replace them with would be a greater hindrance to your spiritual growth than they have been.

"The major point is: Seek Me first with a pure heart and with the energy of a young prince, with boldness and authority and security already in tact, expectantly with thanksgiving already on your lips for the joy and peace that will be your reward.

"In summary, desire Me more than you desire any earthly thing, and you will find yourself investing your time and talents on new and different goals that are rooted in purer values than are presently being espoused."

The Winds Of Revival

"I am speaking at the top of My voice to warn people throughout the world that calamity is about to burst loose on all the earth. Revival is coming, but so is terror from the evil one. Good will be evil spoken of, and good people will be included as topics of evil conversation.

"Be prepared for the hardest days you have ever experienced, remembering always that My promises are still the same. They deliver. They conquer. My voice speaks in and through the storm the same as in the sunshine and harvest times.

"Jesus' Blood is still required to wash the sin stains off of sinners. It will always be needed no matter what circumstances prevail in this life. Point people to Him as their only salvation. Invite them to hear Me speak and hear My voice, for it is calling people even through the raging storms of life.

"The precious Blood of Jesus is still flowing crimson red and purifying people around the globe.

My Spirit is being released in great power like mighty winds. When My breath blows hot, My people yield. They feel it hit the back of their necks, and they stop in their tracks and look around to see what happened. Eventually they look up, for they are expecting the supernatural."

Jesus Is Returning

"Everyone knows or senses that the Lord of Lords is about ready to break the sound barrier and the earth's atmospheric layers to make His appearance in person. Some ignore the signals, but I am faithful in advising My children and in updating their knowledge and understanding.

"Keep working as if He would never return, but know in your hearts that He is returning. Good times are around the corner. First, however, will be hard experiences. Don't be surprised by great persecution. Don't fall away from the faith. You've been warned properly; so don't lose faith that I am in charge and will be the Conqueror, the Almighty King of the Universe.

"Be prepared in every way for the catastrophes coming upon the earth. Don't shake in fear, but rather lift up your head and laugh, praise Me, sing in the Spirit, and dance for joy. Experience the same emotions as those you have at a wedding, for the Bridegroom is on His way, and the ceremony is near at hand.

"The presence of smoke indicates the fact of fire. There is a caldron boiling in this nation. It has been carefully prepared by Satan who thinks he will scald the Christians unto death. But the end will lead to annihilation of the schemer himself. No force or combination of forces can destroy My plan and, therefore, My people. Be prepared, but do not prepare for spiritual death since that is not an alternative for the believer. Jesus is the Victor, and His day of celebration is fast approaching. No armistice signing will accompany this win, for there will be no enemy left to hold the pen at the peace table. I will wipe the earth clean of sin, and for His reign there shall be nothing but love and peace."

Let Not Your Heart Be Troubled

"The monetary system of this world is crumbling. It will not be long until utter chaos will reign. No human mind will be able to solve the problems created by this collapse. Frantic and fearful fighting will occur. Fortunes will be lost overnight.

"Clear thinking and good sense will take its flight, for the security of the hoards will be removed, and there will be nothing to quickly come in and fill the vacuum. Confusion and despair will fill the air. Prepare yourself for this time as best you can, and blindly declare victory through Jesus.

"Hold on to faith in My almighty power. Hold on tenaciously. Let not your heart be troubled. I said, let not your heart be troubled. You cannot know the answers to survival, but you can know the only one true God who does: cling to Me.

"Foreboding times. Ominous wonders. Dreadful scenes. Screaming people. What else do you want to hear about? How much can you take? Listen and I will share with you some secrets of the ages. Harden not your heart, and neither let it be afraid. Strange events to your experience are coming on the earth, but with them will come the opportunity and privilege for you to trust in Me with all your mind and soul and strength. Tenacious faith will see you through. So perhaps it is better to leave it there. Just know in your heart of hearts that you will have the necessary tools of faith to survive anything, for I will not fail to keep My Word. I am not a man that I can lie, and as the Scripture says, I am not the son of man that I should repent. Have I not said it, and will I not carry through on My word? Therefore, go in faith always, and you shall be delivered from the destruction that shall come at noon-day!"

Total Fulfillment

"Peace for all of my children comes in the morning. Morning is now. Peace is meant to be forever. Shallowness of life in Me is an opponent of peace. I work My works best in the lives of My surrendered children. They are too few to please Me.

"My eternal call is to surrender. Surrender totally. With utter abandonment of self. This is the vessel that I can bless and use mightily for My purposes— those purposes which are HIGH ABOVE what mere man can think or design. Fervently seek my mercy that I might graciously share My eternal plan for the unfolding of your life in days ahead.

"Be constant and consistent in your search for Me. My will and My ways are clearly made known to those who yearn to follow Me. The love of earthly fathers is not a suitable comparison for My heartbeat toward My children. The yearning and groaning for My children to find My plan and to obey it has nothing to be compared with—no equal—in human experience. My will is perfect. My plans are extremely appropriate and effective. Desire to know them for yourself. Only then can you feel total in your fulfillment. Only then can you know My peace.

"Forgive. Forget. Redeem the time. Muster new courage. Exhibit new boldness. Jesus Christ is alive within you. Feed your spirits more often with My confirming Word. Relate your present more closely to His future. Become prepared to serve Me now in My Kingdom. He reigns—even now! Envision that Lordship. My plan for you is perfect. My ability to communicate it to you is also perfect. Give high priority to seeking and understanding My will. Magnificent rewards await you."

Hell In Their Hearts

"World peace is a most sought after commodity today. At peace summits, leaders from all over the entire world put their minds to the explosive problems of government and politics. But peace in that realm shall not be found regardless of who meets or for how long. When peace finally flows into the hearts of individual men and women, that is when there shall be peace in the world and not before.

"Don't let yourselves get upset when the headlines boldly announce war. War comes from hell, and when hell remains even in one heart there is the chance for war. So naturally there will be war in the world when there are millions who yet have hell in their hearts.

"Don't fret. Don't get excited. Satan must be bound first, and then peace can come and reign on the new earth. Praise Me that the world does not end with chaos but that sin destroys itself in order to usher in the reign of My government, in which there will be nothing but peace for a season."

Two By Two

"Born-again ones need decision-making instruction more than they need additional, traditional teaching and Bible study. They are fairly well informed about Bible truth, but they are very slack in deciding on specific works of Mine that they must undertake. They pray to be shown, but they fail to connect with the truth that they have already been shown over and over again. Their teaching has not clicked with their need to 'Go thou and do likewise.'

"It is My will for Christians to design a total program of reaching people for Christ. A two-by-two ministry could produce enough new contacts and converts in a few weeks to support healthy new churches. Why do My people not see their own laziness or lack of concern as the reason why the body of Christ is not growing and the present body is so ineffective? Inertia must be replaced by a dynamic plan for witnessing and serving all brethren. This must be a deliberate thing.

"The conviction to be My servant should burn in your hearts with intense heat. Presently you are not on fire to do My work. Being a servant is low on your list of priorities. I won't help that. I can't and be true to My character and plan. It is you who must take the initiative. You must sit down and make the plan and then seek volunteers for working the plan."

Do Something

"Certainly no one needs to tell you what to do. Certainly you are not that hardened and calloused by your desire to do your own thing first and foremost. You see the widows. You see the suffering old people. You see the court records. You read about the single-parent families.

"You know of the crime on the streets and the drinking problem among your youth. Is it the concern only of the secular world? Is that what My Son's life taught you? Are you too good or too 'goodie-good' to want to respond to the human cries for help that are everywhere around you?

"Get involved. Get committed. Get organized. Get on your knees. *Do* something! Stop discussing what's wrong, and begin to demonstrate what is right. Unity will come as you share your experiences and your prayers one with another. I will be close by to help any and all who will put their hand to the plow and begin seeding for a crop."

Reaping The Harvest

"Fruits of the true vine, that variety of God-given fruit that satisfies the belly of all who will heartily eat, is ripening everywhere. There are acres enough for all of My children to gather in a harvest that will satisfy every hunger. Wine flows from the grapes that makes spiritual dining the most nourishing and satisfying experience possible on this planet.

"You are in the very midst of the garden. Reach out on all sides and gather in baskets full of fruit. With it, feed the multitudes around you. Feed My sheep. Nurse My little lambs. Pray prayers for the sick, the lame, the spiritually depressed, the financially cursed. Speak harmony into lives that are experiencing discord. Speak peace to troubled minds and hearts. Fill in the gaps of spiritual knowledge where there is spiritual ignorance.

"Rise, My child, and thresh, for this is the calling unto which you have been chosen. Praise Me that Satan has been defeated. No longer will he torment you in body, soul, or spirit. He has lost his power with you, for I, the Lord God Almighty, am covering you with My very own wings. My wingspread has you in the shadow of My love and power. Evil simply is too feeble to face the light coming forth out of you. He is blinded, and because of this he is in retreat.

"The tools you will need for harvesting are sharpened best on the anvil of My Word. Sharp tools are as necessary when working for a spiritual crop as they are in growing physical food. No harvest of souls is possible without using the instruments of salvation: conviction, convincing, repentance, and faith.

"The plow and planter, the hoe and sickle are all needed, and the sower is responsible for both obtaining the tools and for keeping them sharpened through study and use. Oh, that My children would work harder on their tools of salvation! My gardeners, at best, are only minimally prepared for the great harvest that is fast approaching. Time to sharpen your wits and become fully prepared for the last great ingathering of souls is exceedingly short.

"All time is in concentric circles, speeding in a rapid pace toward the eye of time wherein eternity for all takes on a new meaning and beginning. Rejoice and praise Me, for My eternal plan is progressing on schedule and is exceedingly stable! Mind's eye cannot grasp or the emotions fathom the things that I have planned for those who love Me dearly."

Hope For The Future

After reading these messages, you must realize that God has great things in store for you, both in this life and the next. The best way to be prepared for the future is to be in the center of His will in the present. As you learn to listen to God's voice in prayer, you will know best how to please Him in all you do. Then the future will hold only hope and blessing for your life.

It is my prayer that everyone who reads this book will be challenged to seek the face of God and wait until He speaks. May every voice you hear be only the clear, pure melody of the Father's still small voice. And may your answer always be, "Ah, I hear him—my beloved!" (See Song of Solomon 2:8, *TLB*.)

APPENDIX
Questions And Answers

As I have traveled throughout our nation and in several countries abroad, I have never failed to find believers in Jesus Christ who can share fascinating stories about their direct revelations from God. Hundreds of personal testimonies, plus what the Word says, have convinced me that when a Christian seeks God with all his heart, he finds Him.

Soon after I first began to hear the Holy Spirit's "still small voice," I discovered that many Christians were having this same experience. My scientific mind wanted to investigate this phenomenon, so I designed a questionnaire that could be mailed to other "hearers." With the help of one of my pastors, Herman Riffel, author of the book, *The Voice of God*, I wrote a questionnaire and sent it to one hundred people. Sixty responded to the questionnaire and returned it.

The questions we asked and the answers we received—from people just like you—provide a candid and honest overview of the listening-prayer experience. As you read this appendix, I'm sure you'll be able to identify with many of those who have heard God's voice.

Listening Prayer Questionnaire

1. Can you remember the first time God spoke to you with what you would describe as His "voice"? Please describe.

To this question, a few answered simply "yes," failing to elaborate at all. About half answered "no" but then went on to relate one of the first times that they could remember. Several said that once they began to hear God clearly, they realized that He had been speaking to them all along. Here is a sampling of those who wrote about the first time they heard God speak to them.

> "I had been praying about entering the pastoral ministry and was under great stress concerning the decision. At work one day I couldn't concentrate, so I left my desk and office and went for a walk on the grounds. I cried out to God, 'I must know what you want me to do.' God spoke to me and said, 'I don't want you to *do* anything. I want you.' "

> "Yes, I surely do remember the first time I heard God speak to me. It was during a

church service. I had been trying to give up cigarettes. That evening I said, 'As soon as the pack I bought tonight is gone, I will give them up.' Just then I heard, 'Why not give them up right now?' I looked around but no one was speaking to me. I knew it was God. I never smoked another cigarette nor did I ever want one again!"

Many who answered this question did not report hearing "a voice," but they did report other ways God spoke to them.

"Although I was a baptized Lutheran child, no one had ever told me to consciously give my life to God. When I was about seven years old, I heard the story of Joseph at vacation Bible school. At that time I thought God said to me: 'You are like Joseph—I want you to be pure like him.' It was an inner knowing—a very intimate experience."

"The first time God spoke to me it was through a Scripture verse. As a new Christian, I was in doubt concerning my salvation. I heard, "My Father which gave me them is greater than all and no man can pluck them out of my Father's hand." I knew that word was just for me. Later I began to hear Him speak in many ways—but always in harmony with the Word."

2. At the time God spoke to you, had you been asking God to speak to you or was His speaking a complete surprise from "out of the blue?" How old were you at the time? If you had been asking, what inspired you to do so?

The responses showed that about half were taken by surprise and half were not. One man wrote, "It came as a startling shock." Another man said, "Although I had been quite close to God in spirit and had been seeking direction for my life, I had not even been asking God to speak to me. The voice came out of the blue because I never expected to hear a clear audible voice as such."

The ages at which people started to hear varied greatly—but a large number said they heard as small children. Typical responses were: "All my life;" "Since I was seven;" "After I got saved at fifteen."

All of the answers were interesting. Some people had been encouraged to listen to God while attending Bible college; others from books they read or from watching Christian TV programs.

One cluster of answers to this question centered around their beginning to listen to God because of the examples of others. "My mother" was the most often-mentioned person. One man wrote that he didn't know until after he left home that not every Christian regularly heard from God. It had been such a natural part of his upbringing that he thought everyone had had this experience.

3. To what do you attribute God's having commenced to communicate with you verbally at this particular time?

About one-third indicated that they had just received the baptism of the Holy Spirit. The next most common answer was that it had nothing to do with them but that God had initiated it because He had something to tell them.

Many connected God's beginning to speak with a great problem they were facing—as a response to their own sufferings, doubts, or quandaries. Here are a few of their statements: "My attitude was one of complete brokenness and humility. I needed comforting;" "I was extremely open and hurting;" "I was in my living room crying, and felt like I was at wits-end with myself and the challenge of life."

From this you can see that God met the deep needs of these people when He spoke to them. One man expressed this idea when he wrote, "After I heard Him the first time, I wanted more!"

I like what one person wrote: "I figured if God talked to others and He changes not, then it was true that He still speaks to men today. If He's no respecter of persons, then I knew He would talk to me, too."

4. Describe as exactly as you can the voice with which God speaks to you.

On the whole, most respondents said God does not always speak with an actual voice and that it doesn't always come in the same way. They agreed that God's voice usually seems to come from within themselves—into their "heart" or "spirit" or "soul"—accompanied by an immediate sense of God's presence. It is authoritative, distinct, often comforting, and very moving. Here are some sample responses:

"My listening experience is best described as a *learning* experience. The voice has no sound, yet it moves me more than any voice with sound. I hear it. I receive it within."

"The voice comes from outside myself, mixing into my own thoughts. It is often gentle but firm and direct. All other thoughts are stopped, and I become aware of a specific sentence."

Perhaps this person's answer is most like my own experience, and I believe you will enjoy reading it in its entirety.

"I have heard what I could honestly describe as God's voice perhaps two dozen times in my life. I seemed to receive a message through my ears as speech from an invisible person—and not in the pastor's preaching or through a Christian friend or my own inner voice as I'm reading Scripture.

"But of the times that I have heard a voice through my ear I would have to say that it was almost always with a different quality to the voice each time. I know it's God, not because it 'sounds' a certain way, but because it's so real and affects me so deeply. It always cuts to the very core of my being and is full of revelation.

"Most times I knew for a second or two beforehand that God was about to speak. He causes me to know in my heart that He is going to show me something before He reveals anything special—whether by using a voice or not.

"The atmosphere seems to change or I seem to feel a mild tingling mixed with gratitude and thankfulness for what I know He's about to show me—even when I know it's something about myself that will hurt to face."

I found one point on which all hearers are in agreement: hearing God speak personally is truly wonderful!

5. Does what you describe as "hearing from God" always consist solely of words, or does it sometimes consist of just a few words combined with mental images, impressions, and sensations or sometimes only the latter, with no words at all?

The answers to this question were beautiful. The main point of nearly all of them was that they do not hear solely in words but they hear in all the ways mentioned in the question—and then some! One person's answer was so outstanding I want to include all of it here.

> "While the words themselves can be very simple, God will often apply their meaning simultaneously to several aspects of my life. Or, He will enlighten my mind to be able to understand several very different meanings from one statement as I am hearing it.
>
> "For example: A short time after my father died, I was sitting in the bathtub thinking about how coldly I had always treated him (because of unforgiveness). I was weeping and wishing I had it 'all to do over,' when suddenly I heard very succinct, deliberate, and matter-of-factly: 'Your father's in heaven.' But from those simple words God caused me to instantly understand four separate parallel meanings:
>
> 1. Your dad is with Me up here, and not hurting anymore over how you treated him.
>
> 2. Although you're separated by more physical distance, He's still your dad, and you're still his son. It's not too late for you to honor him with what's left of your life.
>
> 3. I, God, your Heavenly Father, will take over your earthly dad's fatherly role toward you from now on.

4. And by the way, you're not treating Me all that much better than you did your dad!''

6. Does God use your usual vocabulary and sentence structure when He speaks, or does He phrase things differently than you ordinarily would? Does He quote a lot of Scripture? Are you usually familiar with the verses quoted, or not?

The majority answering this question said that they hear God speak in a conversational way that is natural to them. Several said that words are sometimes used which are above their everyday vocabulary but within their comprehension. Many referred to having heard King James scriptures quoted. Two additional features were mentioned with appreciation—God calls them by name, and He sometimes uses a delightful sense of humor. There was great unanimity in the answers to this question—more so than in many others.

An unusual use of language was reported by one person:

"One time the Holy Spirit spoke to me using a foreign language I had studied many years prior to this experience. I had noticed a fleshy deposit like a tumor in my rib-cage area. I was frightened. I heard a voice say 'menaka fotsiny.' I laughed and said to the Lord, 'I won't say anything to the doctor but will see what he says tomorrow.' The next day after a routine exam the doctor said: 'It's only a little extra fat.' That is what the Holy Spirit had told me using the Malagasy words the evening before. I shared it with the doctor and we had a good laugh. This is more than ten years ago, and since then I have had a few physicals and the extra fat is still there but nothing else!''

7. Are you ever uncertain as to whether what you hear is God's voice or your own inner thoughts? Do you feel you ever mix what you genuinely hear from God with your own brainstorms or desires? Has His voice seemed faint at times?

Most everyone who answered this question said that at some time they questioned whose voice they were hearing, especially when they were new listeners. Equally as often they expressed the idea that they soon could recognize God's voice clearly—just as they would a family member's voice. Here are some of the responses.

"I used to feel it was me until I realized I did not have the intelligence to come up with those answers."

"If I am not sure who is speaking, I ask and right away I am told. When I am doing the thinking, my brain seems 'in gear.' When the Holy Spirit is doing the talking, my mind feels 'in neutral'—very relaxed and like a receiver instead of a computer or typewriter!''

"Usually God's message is confirmed either before He speaks or shortly after. I usually feel confirmation within my own spirit. I know that this can be a tricky area, but I do not fear it."

"Because I want to be sure that what I hear is from God, I check it out with those who are more mature in the Lord."

8. For how long at a time does God usually speak? Does He speak continuously or with silences interspersed? How do you know when He has finished speaking?

Many—and mostly men it seemed—never hear more than a sentence or two at once. Their answers generally went something like this: "When God speaks to me, it is very short and to the point."

Others report receiving much longer messages, at least occasionally; and some have long conversations. Here are samples:

"I believe He is always speaking to me. I am always aware of Him being with me and guiding me even when I am cooking. It isn't that His voice is always so clear-cut with a verse or anything, but I sense His leading and His checking what I do."

"Sometimes in short sentences—other times in conversation (in Spirit) until I have all the answers. I know when He has finished because it is all I need to know about that matter. There is always a rest in hearing from Him."

9. How do the ups and downs of your Christian walk correlate with your hearing from God? How does sin in your life bear upon God's willingness to speak?

One thing is certain from the answers received: sin inhibits our hearing from God. Here is a sampling of answers:

"I'm sure God has withheld speaking to me because of sin in my life. When I go for a long time without hearing from Him, I ask Him to reveal any hidden sin in my life."

"The times when I have heard and obeyed the wrong voice were the times I had sin in my life. I prayed as usual thinking I was praying to God, but sin twisted my prayers and I didn't communicate the right message to Him so I didn't receive the right one back. Now I repent *first*."

"My 'ups' are when I am most honest and open with Him. My 'downs' are when I go on my own impulsive impressions. Sin hinders me from hearing from God."

10. Have you ever ignored the counsel or disobeyed a directive that you heard from God? Please elaborate.

There were only two people who said they have never ignored or disobeyed God's voice, one was a simple 'no,' and the other is the first answer below. Only a few who answered 'yes' elaborated at all. Not a popular question I'm afraid.

"I obey God's directives if I have heard Him. If I thought it was God—or was sure it was God—I would certainly obey. The times I probably go my own way is when I haven't been open to His word."

"The very first time I ever heard God I disobeyed Him. As a teenager, sixteen years old, I was strongly impressed by the Lord to witness to a certain person. I procrastinated two weeks. When I drove to his home to obey the Lord, it was too late. This boy had taken his life. I failed in my response to God. This experience was a great lesson, and I have

never again (to my knowledge) disobeyed
the Lord to the point of a soul being lost."

**11. What is most usually the nature of God's
messages to you? (Rebuke, caution, comfort,
encouragement, revelation about yourself or
others, directives, etc.)**

If you ever compose a questionnaire, here's a tip;
don't suggest too many possible answers or you'll
get a lot of "all of the above"; which is how most
everybody answered this question. Here, however,
are some fuller answers:

"He does not 'scold' as such, nor do I
hear specific words of my disobedience.
He treats me this way so as never to 'beat
me down' but to correct me slowly by
change and my desire to please Him. Areas
in which I've been disobedient or that I
need conviction or correction in will just
keep coming up until I know I must repent
or I'll never get past it. God is consistent,
yet gentle.

"He has spoken words of great comfort
to me when I have been at my weakest and
lowest. As the song says, 'He tells me I am
His own,' and He relieves the pressure put
upon me by men's Christian standards. He
lets me know that there's no one I have to
measure up to and that He loves me just as
I am. The words are usually the opposite

of my feelings—if I am weak, He comforts; arrogant, He corrects; critical, He instills compassion.''

"God's usual messages to me are words of encouragement, words of instruction, revelation of things He wants me to incorporate in my lectures, things He wants me to do, people He wants me to contact, poetry for pleasure, and sometimes messages for other people or insights into situations with others, including family members.''

"Much is instruction for daily activities. He will order my day and show me what are His priorities. He will bring to mind people who need prayer or remind me what I am to do. I have been trying to write these instructions down so that I can check my accountability.''

"God has reprimanded me by speaking to me quite a few times. Each time He has made it so clear where my attitude was wrong.''

12. Does God usually introduce surprising and unexpected topics, or does He most often speak to your conscious concerns and questions?

Three-quarters responded like the first answer below.

> "The topics He speaks of are not usually surprising but things He knows I am concerned about and need help with."

13. Do you find God responds more quickly, clearly, or emphatically to certain kinds of questions or areas of concern to you? Which ones?

Most people answered a plain "no." Others said they'd never thought about it but guessed not. The positive responses are all summed-up by the five following examples, with the first being mentioned most often.

> "God answers more quickly during times when I am counseling others and need a word of wisdom, knowledge, or instruction."

> "Yes, questions that involve the apparent contradiction of one part of the Bible with another part."

> "If I go out witnessing to unbelievers, He will always stand with me and bring scriptures to my mind. He surprises me with the answers I find myself giving to their questions—things I never realized myself."

"I find God responds more quickly when I need advice or answers to questions by a certain time."

14. Does God ever/often appoint you tasks you would never have dreamed of undertaking otherwise. Give example(s).

Roughly a third said "no," and a third answered plain "yes." Here are some elaborated yes answers:

"Yes, I am a woman's ministry leader and teacher, and I would never have taken this task if God had not told me to do so."

"He sometimes gives me tasks that I never dreamed of. One time I was sitting in a professional meeting and the Holy Spirit clearly said, 'I want you to write a book for Me.' I would never have undertaken a book even though I had published thirty-seven professional journal articles at the time I heard that voice."

15. Does He ever/often give you precise knowledge you could never have acquired naturally? Give example(s).

"Often when I am counseling or in Bible study and someone asks a question, He gives us the perfect words to say. Many times I will ask a question and wait on the Holy Spirit to give me an answer. I am always amazed at what He gives me that I didn't know."

"Yes, God gives me precise knowledge I could never have acquired naturally."

16. Has God ever summoned you to intercession for causes or persons with whom you have no conscious interest, or even no previous knowledge?

Most everyone answering this question said "yes" they had been summoned to pray for people or causes about which they had no previous knowledge.

17. Has God ever shown you what would come to pass in your life or the lives of others before it did? Things of what sort? Why do you think He did? Has God ever shown you future events of a more general and remote nature?

The majority answered "yes" to this question. A few examples follow:

"When I was teaching a Bible class to a rather mature group of people with a mixed background, I bought all kinds of books as aides and was spending much time with these books. Then one night I had a dream that I got up in church to read the Bible, but

I couldn't find it anywhere and didn't have a thing to read. This showed me that I had better get back into the Bible and spend most of my preparation time there."

"When He speaks to me about the future it mainly is just to trust in Him, do what He says, and when I need to know something He will tell me. In a rather veiled way, He has led me to prepare for the future and caused me to buy things to be ready for an emergency."

"Yes, the Lord showed me something that was going to come to pass that was dangerous and frightening. In dreams He showed me and both of my children on the same night. It was a treacherous situation that came to pass exactly as we had dreamed. If we had not been warned, the end could have been tragic. God showed us His mercy and concern for our lives. When we were in danger, He wanted all of us to know that He was in charge and would give us the protection we needed."

18. Has God ever revealed to you things you wish He hadn't. Have you ever asked Him NOT to tell you certain things? Have you ever asked Him to please stop speaking?

"No, God has not revealed to me anything that I wish He hadn't. His promises to me have been so wonderful that they keep me 'bated for new fish' all the time. Miracles are constantly happening to us, and I expect them to continue on the basis of what the Holy Spirit has shared with us."

"God keeps bringing me back to His priorities, and why I move ahead without proper order. Other times when He gave insight into something that was not pleasant or edifying, I still appreciated it because I knew it was His will and He was in control."

"The things I hear from Him that I need to act upon come first as an inner voice from within and as a sudden revelation. I usually don't act on these right away because they are normally against my own will. But in time, it will keep coming up over and over till I know I must act on it or not grow in Him."

19. Do you believe you have ever heard Satan or demons while listening for God? Did they try to impersonate God and deceive you by imitating His voice, or did they address you forthrightly, not attempting to conceal their identity? How can a listener protect himself from being confused by demons?

"I don't think Satan can fool a mature Christian very long. You soon recognize that what is being said is out of character with God. You can protect yourself from that by binding Satan, his demons and their fruits from interfering while you are in listening prayer. Command your mind to be quiet and inactive, and command Satan to be silent. This has helped me."

"I feel we can protect ourselves by being led by the Holy Spirit and judging it by the Word and prayer."

"Over the years I have learned to be more discerning and to check things out by putting them on the shelf until the Lord confirms them. It is also important to submit things to my spiritual brothers and sisters."

20. Have you ever been sure you heard from God on a matter and then later realized that it was not Him you heard? How did you realize it? How do you account for your mistake?

"No, I've not experienced that. When I am *sure* I've heard His voice, I never question whether it was Him or not. Instances where I *think* I'm hearing Him (and it's not in the specific, audible voice), I have often been wrong. I realize my mistake when things no longer go smoothly."

"When I was carried away by my emotions or acted out of sympathy or pity, I have later realized that my heart has deceived me."

"Yes, I have heard on several occasions what I thought was the Holy Spirit and later realized it wasn't. I was 'checked' in my spirit soon after I began to hear in each instance. I did realize it after a moment or two. Then there are other times that I feel my own thoughts got mixed in and I wrote down my big ideas instead of the Holy Spirit's. I believe God will protect me when I need it; He will teach me when I need it; He will forgive me when I need it; and He will love me for my honesty in wanting to follow as closely to Him as I possibly can! He knows my heart. It is deceitful, but my life is in His hands and I know He won't let me fall!"

21. Do you ever, usually, or always seek confirmation on what you hear? How?

"On receiving the word to go to Saudi Arabia, we knew God confirmed it in both of us. The pastor and other elders did not receive this as being from God, so we asked God to confirm it in His Word. When I was visiting a friend, her Bible was open to Galatians 1:17, *New English Version* and I read: 'Without consulting the elders Paul went away to Arabia.' (Later I found this was the only version that reads this way.) Praise God for His Word. If He sends, He protects."

"I almost always seek confirmation on what I hear before I act on it. I get confirmation from Scripture, my church leaders, prayer partners, and I always try to make sure it fits into the guiding of the overall church."

22. Do you ever share your messages with others? Under what circumstances do you share or not share with others? Have you always asked God's okay? How do most people with whom you share a message respond? Is their response usually negative or positive? Give examples. Have you ever shared when you shouldn't have?

Of every question I asked, this one solicited the fullest responses. Absolutely no one failed to elaborate their answer. I think this is because almost everyone has been hurt trying to share their hearing experiences with others.

"People made me feel like they resented my hearing from God, and not them. I have learned to share only with the people the Lord guides me to share with."

> "After much disappointment and hurt, I've learned to tell only those who understand."

People listed many reason's for sharing: to acknowledge Him before others, to edify the body, to seek confirmation, to encourage others to seek the Lord, to deliver a message they believe God gave them for another, to seek help interpreting what they hear, and "just to share."

> "I usually share it with my wife, then my pastor. If they feel positive about it, I share it with our staff and let them pray about it. Almost always it proves to be of God."

23. Do you have a special way of preparing yourself spiritually for listening?

Close to 85 percent said to hear from God with any regularity they did need to prepare themselves for listening. First I will offer a few typical responses in whole, and then I will break the remainder down into their most common components.

> "Before I ask the Lord anything I always ask Him to help me 'die' to my thoughts, desires and imaginations (Isaiah 55:8; 2 Corinthians 10:5) and deal aggressively with the enemy in the powerful name of Jesus! (James 4:7; Zechariah 3:2)"

"I listen after my devotions. In between I'll read a Psalm out loud or sometimes sing and then stop to remember how He has answered my prayers and thank Him. Before I wait on God about anything, I always pray in tongues knowing in that way He will cause me to ask for what He wants me to ask for."

"Before I start my day I praise Him, confess my sins, ask His blessing on my day, pray for others, and then listen."

"Yes, I have a special way of preparing myself for listening. I pray in my prayer closet by singing, reading, praying, interceding, and writing inspired things. Then when I am ready to listen, I command Satan to stay out. Then I quiet my mind and tell the Holy Spirit He is welcome to speak. I ask Him a question or two by writing it on the top of a page of clean paper, and then I get quiet and listen."

Most people who answered set aside time daily to be still before the Lord as part of their "devotions" or "quiet time."

Nearly everyone preceded their listening with time in the Word. Also frequently mentioned were singing, praising God, walking and praying, walking and observing nature, praying in tongues, and reflecting on what the Lord has done for them already. Several, before beginning to listen, write in their notebooks what they are thinking or praying about. But other than time in the Word, the three most popular preparations cited were these:

1. Getting right with God.
2. Getting tough with the Devil.
3. Getting quiet within.

24. Are there any particular things you routinely ask of God before you begin waiting for Him to speak?

Most people said "no." Several said they ask the Lord to not let them be fooled by Satan or led away with their own thoughts. Several said they ask Him to show them any sin in their lives. Here are two answers I liked that were a little different.

> "I ask the Father, Son, and Holy Spirit to allow me to come into their presence."

> "I ask Him to clear the air of any doubts, fears, and judging or critical thoughts."

25. Do you have a regular time for listening? Describe your usual pattern.

I hope everyone agrees that "the time of the day" is not the most important part and that we should try all day every day to be attuned to God's voice. Nevertheless nearly everyone did have a regular pattern of listening. Perhaps two-thirds listen in the morning, and the other one-third at night. Here are some examples:

"At the beginning of the day and many times during the day. I like to have a good quiet time early in the morning before I see people."

"In the morning after my family is gone."

"Early every morning, but the best seems to be on my days off and/or weekends."

"My lunch hour from work seems to be my special time and the place is down by the river."

"In the car while driving I often get the answer that early morning listening did not bring."

"I pray mornings, but I'm too anxious to get on with the day to be quiet then. If I wait till bedtime, I start dozing off. So I set aside time when I get home from work or after supper."

"After my child is asleep, and prime time is in the middle of the night when all is quiet."

26. Do you have a prayer closet or special place for listening?

Eighty-five percent who answered that they do have a special place for listening can be grouped into three main categories. Thirty-five percent listen in an actual closet they've set aside for that purpose, 35 percent have "prayer closets" that are not literal closets, and 15 percent use several special places, usually depending on who else is home. Here are some specific answers to the question.

> "I shut the bedroom door when the kids are home. My husband uses his shop in the basement as his prayer closet, and I sometimes go down there, too."

> "I have a place, but the Lord told me that I was becoming conditioned to only hearing from Him in my special prayer room. He said that He wanted me to know I could commune anytime, anywhere—that I was continually in the Holy of Holies."

> "My study, a room especially dedicated to God's work, and my kitchen table—my favorite spot since I live alone."

27. Do you have trouble keeping your mind concentrated on listening while you wait? If so, how do you bring your mind back to listening?

"What God says to me has my entire attention because He tells me things I would not know otherwise."

"Looking over the times I've heard Him, I can't say that I've purposed to hear Him— the answer or word just came while I sat quietly listening to nature, thinking thoughts of Him."

"I've learned how to tune out, knowing there is nothing more important. As a young Christian I didn't know that if you were interrupted you could go back and the Holy Spirit would take up where you had to leave off."

"If I'm just casually having time with the Lord and the thoughts of the day intrude, I write them on a notepad that I keep handy during prayer time. I trap the thoughts on paper so they can't be used by the enemy as a distraction."

28. How long after you invite God to speak to you do you usually have to wait for Him to do so? Does it greatly vary?

One thing's for sure, we don't have a cookie-cutter God! Here are a few answers. You're welcome to try and categorize them, I give up.

"Sometimes quickly, other times I have to wait, and there have been times I thought He was not going to answer at all."

"It usually comes quietly after I have read His Word and taken time to meditate on a portion."

"It is very rarely immediately and often in unexpected ways. Sometimes the answer simply comes in my own awareness."

29. Does God ever withhold answering specific questions by telling you that you shouldn't have asked, or by silence?

All respondents said that, on occasion, God had denied the answer to certain questions. Here are some sample responses:

"Sometimes by silence."

"Yes, God, does withhold answering many times. No, He never has told me I shouldn't have asked. Yes, there is silence many times. I stay at rest during times of silence."

"God doesn't answer every question when I ask. He may answer it at some time—but not always. I wanted to know when my kids would be saved, but He never told me—just that they were coming closer to hearing His voice."

"I don't ask questions I know are none of my business. If I ask one by mistake, I quickly find out. There are times I don't have a concrete answer—in words—just the sense that I'm to trust and not be disturbed."

30. Do you keep a journal of what you hear? Do you write while you are listening or later? Do you type it or tape it? Elaborate.

Roughly half of those answering keep some kind of a record. I'll let a few of those who don't, speak first:

"No, I have never kept a log of what I hear from the Holy Spirit although many times I have written down much of what has happened in answer to prayer—truths He has given me and lessons I have learned, etc. Also, I have written down answers to prayer and when I had prayed the prayers."

"I do not keep a journal of what I hear, but usually remember it accurately. If I write anything, I generally do it later."

"I keep a list of important experiences, miracles, revelations, visions, dreams, etc."

"I try to keep a daily log which I treasure greatly. He has become not only my Savior but my teacher and dearest friend. He enjoys pouring out His heart to His children."

"Yes, and I read it over and over until it becomes a part of my spirit."

31. Do you hear from God more clearly, more often, about more things, and more quickly now than when you first began listening?

Finally we have a consensus on something, and I'll let one respondent answer for them all:

"Not counting my 'honeymoon' period after I was saved or the time right after I was filled with the Spirit, yes, I hear from God more clearly, more often, and about more things than when I first began listening."

32. Has your insight into the character and ways of God changed in any way as a result of your hearing?

"Yes, I used to think of God as a 'killjoy,' but I don't anymore. I used to have fears about what He would ask me to do and sometimes I still have some fears, but I know they are unfounded."

"I used to view Him as an ancient, distant, unrelating, severe God. Now I have a relationship with a caring, loving, concerned, gentle Father."

"Yes, I have definitely learned that God's ways are not our ways. I no longer try to bring Him to my level, but I try to go to His level. Suffering and defeat used to seem to me something to pray to be removed very quickly, but if we allow God to work through these types of things far greater lessons can be learned."

33. What impact has your listening had on your Christian growth and development?

"Very much. But it's more than hearing from God, the important thing is obeying after we've heard."

"I feel much closer to God, trust Him more and love Him more."

"I have gained great confidence and come up out of a world of low-self-esteem by the realization that God speaks to me."

"This experience has expanded my spiritual growth. I know Him better, and He has become more of a person to me. I can tell others more about Him too."

34. Do you believe hearing from God personally is a promise that can be appropriated by every believer? Based on what? Why do you believe more Christians do not hear from God in this way?

"Yes, I believe hearing from God personally is a promise that every believer can enjoy. I don't believe I am any more spiritual or loved any greater than anyone else. As a loving and kind Father, I'm sure He would want all His children to hear Him clearer."

"Yes, I believe that all can hear from God personally because His Word says so— Romans 12:2, 1 Corinthians 2:6-16; 3:16, 2 Corinthians 3:3,12ff, and Ephesians 1:17ff."

34. What advice or "tips" would you suggest to the beginner in listening?

"I would tell a beginner to be honest with the Lord, tell Him their real thoughts, longings, goals and joys. Ask Him to open their ears and eyes. Also and not last—to believe."

"Do not become discouraged if it takes too long. Have faith that God is there and will speak to you. Step out in faith. Don't be afraid to make mistakes. Take time. Quiet yourself, and write down what you hear."

"Pick a special time everyday to be alone with Him, in a quiet setting. Read the Word first; acknowledge that He is there with you; then sit quietly thinking about Him and praising Him for His majesty and His goodness; feel yourself draw into Him deep within yourself and meditate. Do not hold back any part of yourself from Him and picture Him right there beside you."

"Love the Lord with all your heart—worship and acknowledge Him as King of Kings and Lord of all—creator and controller of all. Expect Him to move at all times and direct your path as you yield to Him to be led by His Spirit."

"After hearing God's voice, confirm it or wait for confirmation. Submit it to another committed believer who also hears from God."

I hope the responses to this questionnaire have helped answer some of your questions about how God speaks to His children today. I would be glad to hear from you regarding your personal experiences with listening prayer and how hearing the voice of God has changed your life.

ABOUT THE AUTHOR

Mary Ruth Swope received a Bachelor of Science degree from Winthrop College, Rock Hill, South Carolina, a Master of Science degree in Foods and Nutrition from the Woman's College of the University of North Carolina, Greensboro, and a doctorate from Teacher's College, Columbia University, New York City.

After seven years of high school teaching in Vocational Home Economics programs, Dr. Swope served as a nutritionist with the Ohio Health Department. She then joined the Foods and Nutrition faculty at Purdue University and later served as Head of Foods and Nutrition at the University of Nevada.

As a college administrator, Dr. Swope served as Head of Home Economics at Queens College, Charlotte, North Carolina, and Dean of the School of Home Economics, Eastern Illinois University, Charleston, Illinois, for eighteen years.

Dr. Swope and her husband, Don, took early retirement to begin a new ministry, *Nutrition With A Mission*. Through lectures and seminars, they encourage their audiences to deny themselves unneeded calories, save the money the calories would have cost, and give it to Great Commission projects. Her bestselling title, *Are You Sick & Tired of Being Sick & Tired,* is a scripturally oriented nutrition sourcebook and contains sound dietary guidelines, spiritual nourishment, and delicious recipes.

Dr. Swope is a popular lecturer who has been a seminar speaker at PTL in Charlotte, North Carolina and Christian Retreat in Bradendon, Florida. She has also made many television and radio appearances, including the *700 Club* on the Christian Broadcasting Network; TBN's *Joy; It's A New Day; Today, the Bible, & You;* the *Southwest Radio Church;* etc.

Dr. Swope's current address is P.O. Box 1746, Melbourne, Florida 32901.